Tackle Ski-ing

Douglas Godlington

Tackle SKI-ING

Stanley Paul · London

Stanley Paul & Co. Ltd.
3 Fitzroy Square, London W 1

An imprint of the Hutchinson Group

London Melbourne Sydney Auckland
Wellington Johannesburg Cape Town
and agencies throughout the world

First published 1973
© Douglas Godlington

Set in Monotype Ehrhardt
Printed in Great Britain by
The Stellar Press Ltd
Welham Green, Hatfield, Herts.

ISBN 0 09 117720 0 (cased)
      0 09 117721 9 (paper)

Contents

Introduction

A winter sports holiday is now within the reach of everyone. The rise in popularity of ski-ing as a sport has led to the development of many new ski areas and as a result the cost of a ski holiday has been tailored to suit most people's pockets. Learning to ski has also undergone many changes since the first organised ski classes in the Arlberg Technique by Hannes Schneider. Equipment, too, has now made it possible for the enthusiast to learn to ski much more quickly than even a few years ago. The mountains are still there in all their beauty, and there is nothing to compare with a leisurely ski down through the silence of thick sparkling snow. The whole family can enjoy the stay in the clean air of a winter resort, you don't *have* to ski – there are always plenty of other activities available to keep you busy. But if you are at all in reasonable physical shape, you should give ski-ing a try, and once you have got over the first steps you will become smitten with ski fever like all the other skiers around the world!

Over the past few years, the basic techniques of ski-ing control, as taught by the many different countries offering ski holidays, have gradually emerged into a similar pattern. Accordingly there is now very little difference in the methods by which you will be taught to ski, no matter which ski resort you choose for your holiday. In the search to make ski-ing easier, the use of the shorter ski over the unwieldy standard length of ski is the most encouraging development over recent years.

This book describes the basic technique, together with that of more advanced ski-ing, that in the practical way you will need to apply when you get to your ski resort. The technique has been described in as simple terms as is possible, so that you can learn the progression easily and get the feeling of being actually on the snow – what you will have to do, or meet and watch out for, when ski-ing down a slope. Practice the various progressive manoeuvres until you feel that you can manage each one without difficulty – perfection is not necessary. If it feels right and the skis are doing what you want them to do, then you have it in rough controlled form at least. Everyone cannot ski in exactly the same way. You will develop your own ski-ing style because of the differences in physical make-up from person to person. The use of ski lifts is all part of the business of learning to ski, and this is dealt with in the way that you will meet them in practice. Ski-ing technique is too often talked about in cold academic terms, and usually relates the various manoeuvres to smooth untrodden snow, whereas in actual fact when you ski down a run or piste no two turns are ever the same as the snow and terrain are constantly changing. I have attempted to take you out on to the snows of a typical ski resort and give you exactly the same lessons that you will take in a ski class, or with me for private instruction! Safety is of prime importance, as this also relates to the enjoyment of learning to ski. There are certain 'rules of the road' to observe, as well as many other tips in the craft of becoming a competent skier. It is now possible to become 'exercised' into the feel of ski-ing before going on holiday, by the use of artificial ski slopes, and the skier should take every advantage of these facilities in order to use the holiday time to the maximum.

Finally it is intended that this book should accompany you when you go to buy or choose equipment, and should certainly go with you when you take your ski holiday. It is hoped that the suggestions given here will make ski-ing for you all the more enjoyable.

1 · On the Nursery Slope

Before you can ski there is the important matter of equipment. You may have borrowed skis from a friend or bought a second-hand pair. If this is the case the chances are that the skis are far too long. If you are buying or renting a pair ensure that they are no longer than 175 cms. for a medium height person, or 190 cms. for taller people. Children should not use skis longer than their own height. So much depends on starting off correctly and enjoying ski-ing that it is wrong to put beginner skiers on long or 'standard' skis. Already many ski schools are using a short ski method of introducing newcomers to the sport, and as the new equipment replaces the existing rental arrangements, then this way of graduating the length of ski according to the ability of the student will become universal. In Austria, the 'father' of modern ski techniques, Professor Stefan Kruckenhauser, has recommended that beginners are taught the basics using only a 150 cms. long ski, progressing to practice the more advanced ski-ing manoeuvres on 175 cms. skis.

Ski bindings consist of a toepiece and some mechanical means of holding the heel of the boot. Some bindings are designed so that you simply step in and press the heel down, in order to fasten the ski to the boot. Other heel devices require pressing or pulling on by hand. The older type of cable and lever binding should be carefully checked to ensure that the cable is able to slide along the guides on the side of the ski. For your own safety, ask to be shown the adjustment and setting of the release mechanism of the binding. Ski poles should be long enough to

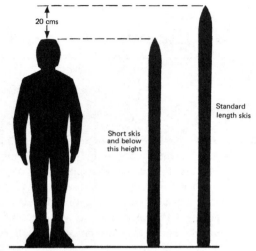

20 cms

Standard
length skis

Short skis
and below
this height

Choosing a ski length

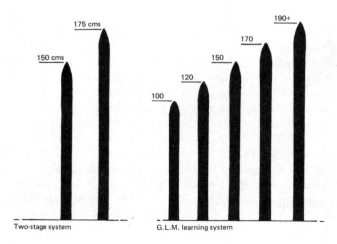

175 cms

150 cms

Two-stage system

190+

170

150

120

100

G.L.M. learning system

Figure 1.

10

Figure 2. *Ski boot and binding attachments.*

reach comfortably to just under the armpit, or about 10 cms. less than this measurement.

Ski boots are perhaps the most important part of a skier's equipment, and it is most essential that they fit snug and firm on the foot. Having a loose fitting boot means that feeling between the foot and the ski is less sensitive. Modern ski boots are made in a waterproof plastic material for the outer shell, with inners that can be shaped or moulded to give a soft snug lining for the

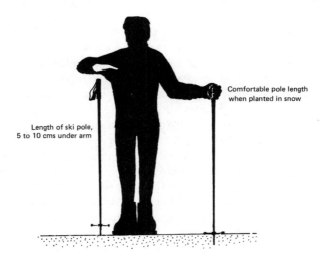

Figure 3. *Ski pole length.*

foot profile, leaving the toes free to wriggle. The design of ski boots allows for the ankle to be bent forward, but rigidly supports the foot against bending sideways. Extremely high backed boots are for advanced ski-ing, although a small shaped support to the back of the boot can be useful and helpful for balance control. Whether you buy a new pair of boots, or hire them for your first ski-ing attempt, be absolutely certain that they fit correctly and comfortably – don't accept the first pair you are fitted with if you are not sure that they feel just right.

Fundamentals of ski-ing

Ski-ing is the motion of travelling over snow. It requires a certain basic understanding of things that you can do, and other things that you cannot do. The first fundamental difference to become familiar with is that of the feet sliding and pushing along the sole of the foot instead of rolling, lifting and stepping from heel to toe. The foot has to adapt to a new feeling of pressure points in order to correct the skier's balance and manoeuvre controls. The beginner's first hurdle, then, is to accept the limitations of leg action that the wearing of skis presents, learning how these limitations can be used to perform ski technique movements. On flat snow the skier provides his own locomotion, pushing each foot and ski as if they are a sliding platform along their separate paths, helped by the poles either to push or to correct any loss of balance. The boot and ski can only be lifted and stepped forward or to the side. Once the skier begins to slide down a slope, then gravity provides the locomotion force, and the control of the speed downhill is made by holding the skis at an angle across the slope. This calls for a change in the sliding feel of the skis. To brake and slow down or stop, as well as make any turning movements, the skier has to be able to press his weight down through specific parts of the feet and boots on to the skis, instead

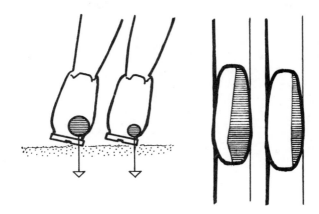

Figure 4. Pressure points on the foot to control ski edging.

of evenly spreading the weight pressure all over the foot as when sliding on the flat. Leaning forward, to the side or slightly backwards keeps the centre of gravity over the skis in order to stand up in balance. Bending and stretching of the body and legs also affect the skier's balance control, or change the weight pressure on the skis to help in turning or slowing the skis down. The length of the skis help with the fore and aft stability, with the arms and poles helping balance sideways.

Pleasure ski-ing downhill is performed by the experienced skier as a graceful series of movements – turning for control in short quick turns to negotiate narrow or steep places, then using long wide turns to sweep across open easy slopes, and stopping by turning the skis up into the slope. All ski turns are different, and there are many ways in which to execute them, but ski-ing uses a combination of whole body movements all the time. This makes for rhythm in the movements that the skier makes in using ski technique, the body is in constant motion as the skis are steering in the direction you want them to go.

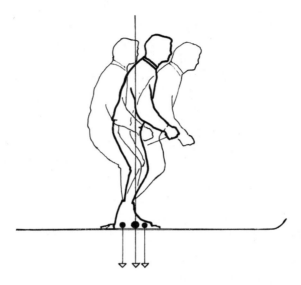

Figure 5. Effect of forward and backward lean on foot pressure points.

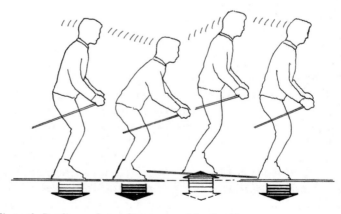

Figure 6. Bending and stretching to unweight the skis.

14

In ski-ing the lower part of the body has most of the work to do, using leg play to turn the skis, while the upper body is held in a relaxed natural posture using a minimum of movement to stay in balance. The legs absorb the terrain. By acting like the shock absorbers of a car over bumps and hollows, they generate the force to turn the skis, and by bending the joints they give control of the ski edges. Turning and traversing down the pleasure ski runs of modern ski areas, the legs then play the most important part of the action, the bending and flexing of the ankles and knees being essential points in ski technique. Rhythm of movements is acquired by practice. Then the skier can combine and direct the movements smoothly in a relaxed balanced slide, avoiding any jerky or stiff actions of the legs and body that could interfere with the rhythm.

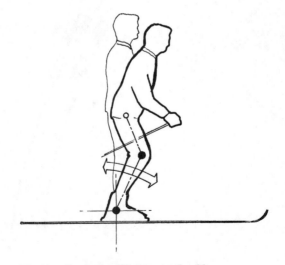

Figure 7. Hinging effect by bending knees and ankles.

15

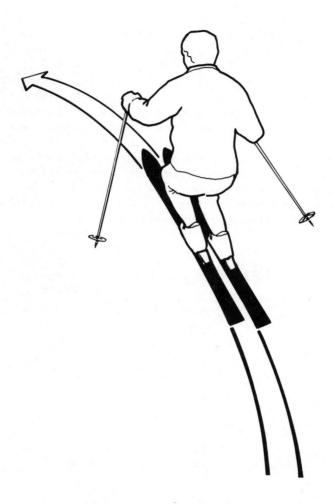

Figure 8. Curved shape of ski helps in turning and steering control.

Finally the actual shape of the skis plays an important part in the turning or skidding of the skis in a curving path across the snow. The curved shape of the sides and the flexing of the ski from tip to heel, helps to carve the skis into the turns.

Getting the feel of skis

No matter how eager you are to put your skis on and have a go at ski-ing – feeling the dream come true, perhaps, of skis swishing through powder snow – you will have to carry the skis and poles to the spot where the first lesson begins. It may not be very far, but even so there is a wrong and right way of comfortably carrying the equipment. Skis can be very awkward things to lug around, never mind when they are fixed to your feet. It is essential to carry skis correctly, both for your own comfort and for other people's safety. In crowded places, as when queuing for cable cars, in airport terminals or railway stations, care must be taken in the way you carry the skis, so as to avoid accidentally hitting other travellers with them.

Place the ski soles, the running surfaces, together, with the bindings to the outside. Clip the tips together with a rubber strap, or tie the skis in the middle with the retaining straps. In this way the skis are prevented from slipping apart and becoming clumsy things to manage. Lift the skis up on to your shoulder, to balance them at the middle, holding the tips forward and down. Hold the forepart to steady the skis, leaving the other hand free to carry both poles or to use them as walking sticks. Once you have reached the nursery slope, pick out a flat area and place the skis down side by side on the snow. Don't throw the skis down on to the snow, they may slide off! Plant your poles on either side level with the bindings. If there is even just a small incline to the snow surface the skis will tend to slide off downhill – don't forget that is what they are made for! Should you

Figure 9. Carrying skis.

Slope fall-line

Figure 10. Putting skis on.

18

have to put your skis on while standing on a slope, place one ski firmly into the snow, either by sticking the heel down into the snow, or by turning the ski over on its upper surface. Then you can fix on the ski on the downhill side first. This makes it much easier to put on the other ski. Assuming that the skis are lying on a flat area, first of all just recheck that the bindings are free to operate, and if necessary readjust the mechanism to ensure that they will release your boot should you take a tumble. Most bindings are clearly marked as to which is the lightest setting, which is the one you will require to begin with. Place the boot into the toebinding squarely, so that the boot and ski are in line with one another. Press the heel down into the heelbinding, or fix on with your hand the binding that secures the heel of the boot down on to the ski. Strap or clip on the retaining straps, which are necessary to stop the ski from running off when the boot is released from the ski in the event of a fall. Take hold of the poles by slipping the hand up through the strap loop, gripping the pole handle and the strap in the palm of the glove.

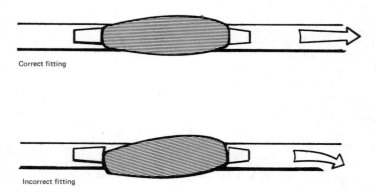

Correct fitting

Incorrect fitting

Figure 11. Fixing boots square into bindings.

19

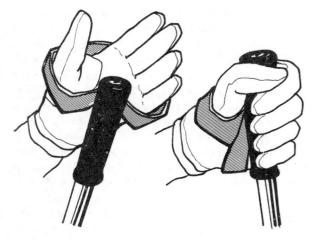

Figure 12. Correct way of holding ski poles.

If the skis are tilted over and not flat it will be difficult to get the boot to fit snugly into the bindings. Tamp out a flat area with the ski if necessary. It is also very important that all the snow is removed from the soles of your boots before attempting to put the skis on. Hard packed snow on the soles can be removed by turning one ski over on its side, and using the steel edge as a scraper to clean off the snow.

Having fixed the skis on securely, the first exercises are made on the spot to get the feel of the skis. Lift first one ski off the snow and swing the tip from side to side, supporting yourself with the poles. Then replace that ski alongside the other, and picking up the other do the same lift and swing movement. Three or four swings out and across the other ski will give you an idea of how heavy the skis are, and how turning the toes in or out very slightly, makes quite a big angle at the ski tip. Now slide the skis backwards and forwards on the spot, shoot one leg forward and slide the other back, again holding on to the poles. Feel how slippery the skis are as they slide on the snow. Lift only the heel of one ski off the snow, leaving the tip down. Step the foot out to the side and place the ski down at an angle. Place the poles well out to the side, and lift the other ski in alongside. Carry on stepping round, first one ski then the other until you have gone completely round in a circle. This is called a Star Turn because the pattern left in the snow is like a many pointed star shape. Remember you can only step the outside ski to the side. Trying to step with the left ski to go to the right will cross the heel or tip over the other ski, and is an example of an easy mistake to make. Don't make too big a step to start with, clocking the skis round from the tips. Step round in both directions, then try lifting the tips off the snow and keeping the heels down at the centre of the turn. Practice the Star Turn until you are quite sure that the awkward length of the skis is becoming more familiar, and that apart from your toes suddenly having grown about one metre in front of you, there are also behind you two long lengths of ski that can easily snag up in the snow and cross over each other. Staying on the flat part of the slope, slide the skis forward one at a time, pushing with the poles, until you are walking and sliding with legs and arms swinging in rhythm with one another, as you do normally when walking along. Try not to lift the skis off the snow, but shuffle the feet to bend the knees forward, giving an occasional push with both poles at once until the skis glide along together for a short distance. Turn round while you are still on the flat slope by using the Star Turn as before. If you have plenty of space to walk around on then try walking and stepping the skis out to the side, to slide and walk round in a circle, until you have become fully accustomed to step and slide the skis forward.

Before you can attempt a slide down even the smallest slope, you will have to learn how to climb uphill. If you simply point

Walking action

Use of double-pole push to glide

Figure 13. Walking and gliding steps.

the skis up the slope, and try to walk uphill, you will only go for
a short distance before the skis will slide backwards. However,
if you step the skis so that they are parallel across the line of the
slope – horizontal to the angle of the hill – the skis will not slide.
In addition the skis have to be tilted over to make the ski sole
bite its own step into the snow, to prevent the whole ski sliding
sideways down the slope, as will happen when the skis are kept

22

Figure 14. Star turn to step round.

Figure 15. Side-stepping up a slope.

flat on the snow. This is the one of the basic principles of ski technique, controlling and feeling the correct amount of tilt you apply through the boots to the skis, in order to bite the ski edges into the snow. To climb uphill the skis are sidestepped, holding their horizontal position across the snow. The ski on the uphill side has its ski sole metal outer edge pressed into the snow, the knee being pressed towards the slope so as to cant the ski and make a step platform in the snow. The ski on the down side has its inside edge pressed into the snow in the same manner. Think in terms of the outside edge of the skis being under the little toe, and the inner ski edge below the big toe. In this way it is easier to envisage which is the respective side of the foot on which to press. Sidestepping uphill uses a press on to the little toe side of the foot as the upper ski is stamped into the snow. Then the lower ski has a push off the big toe inner edge to lift and press the ski in alongside the upper one. Plant the poles out to the side in line with the front of your boot, holding on to them for balance while you step the skis. The slope is ascended in a series of sidesteps and ski edging. Step uphill, bring lower ski together, move the poles, step uphill and bring lower ski together – stamping the skis into the snow if the surface is hard. The stepping is just the same as if you were climbing up a staircase sideways, one step at a time, and this is the pattern that you leave in the snow. It is sometimes more comfortable to climb up the slope in an ascending traverse. To do this diagonal step, the normal walking action is combined with the side-stepping movements: lifting the uphill leg and stepping it forward by bending the knee forward as well as in towards the slope, again pressing on the little toe to grip with the upper ski edge. With the help of a push off the pole, the lower ski is stepped up parallel, pressing the big toe ski edge into the snow. Walking and stepping to press the ski edges into the slope, use a smooth action with the legs and arms. Be sure to keep the skis always

Step turn

Kick turn

Figure 16. Stepping round on a slope.

25

across the slope, not lifting the tip or heels higher than the rest of the ski. When you want to turn round and face the opposite direction, then the skis have to be stepped round as in the Star Turn on the flat. The difference now is that you have to support yourself on the poles in order to stop yourself sliding backwards or forwards. To get the best support, it is necessary to change the grip on the pole handles. The palm of the hand is placed on the top of the handle to push down on the pole with the arms straight. You can step round either facing down the slope or the other way, looking up the hill. To step round facing up the slope is less tiring on the arms, lifting the tips of the skis round one at a time. As the skis are gradually turned across the slope, you will have to change the pressure over from one side of the foot to the other, since the edges are made to bite into the snow.

You can also climb up gentle slopes by facing uphill, opening the tips out in a V form, and walking up the slope by holding the tips apart and the heels together, pressing on both big toes to stamp the inside edges of the skis in order to get a grip on the snow. The pole is planted just behind the boot to push off and stop any tendency for the ski to slide backwards.

The first slide downhill

Choose a gentle slope that has a flat area at the bottom, large enough for you to allow the skis to run out and stop. Climb up about 10 metres and while holding on the poles planted on the lower side, step round until both skis are pointing straight down the slope. Keep the feet apart, about the width of your hand, say 10 to 15 cms. approximately. This is called the Open Skis position. Bend the knees and ankles forward, towards the ski tips, so that if you look down you will see that your knees are in line with the end of your boots. Once you feel ready to start, have a quick look round to see that no one is in the way or about to

Figure 17. Herringbone climbing step.

Figure 18. Holding on poles ready to ski downhill.

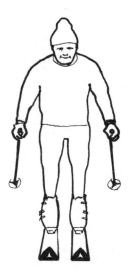

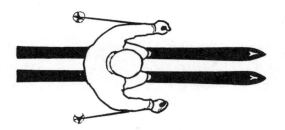

Figure 19. Straight-running position.

ski across your path. Let the skis slide, lifting the poles out of the snow and allowing them to trail behind you. Keep the knees pressed forward so that you stay in balance, because straightening the legs will throw you back on your heels and the skis will speed up, with the result that you will sit backwards into the snow. Allow the skis to slide out on to the flat part at the bottom, until they slow down and stop of their own accord. Go back up the slope and repeat these small straight runs several times, always keeping the legs flexed with a loose springy action. Look down the slope as you slide, so that at the same time you are just able to see your hands held comfortably forward, not tightly held into the waist. Be sure to hold your poles with the points facing backwards, so that they are out of the way of becoming snagged in the snow. The more of these short runs you do the better, but make certain that the track is always clear before you start, and do not try too steep a hill because the speed will be too fast for you to feel relaxed over the skis. After a while you will feel confident to test and try the limitations of movements you can make while sliding along. Bend down to touch the toe piece of the ski bindings with your hand, then stand up again, repeating the up and down bending as you slide. Try lifting the heel of one ski while sliding, then put the ski back down parallel, and lift the other ski. Eventually you can make a small side step with one ski, opening the parallel track wider, and then stepping in the other ski, so that you have moved your line downhill over to one side. This can be done to the opposite side, until it is possible to change the direction by using small stepping movements. The important thing to remember is not to make hurried jerky bending or stepping actions, but a smooth deliberate movement without being stiff or rigid. If you find that you are tensed up, take a deep breath and slowly exhale before you start, or even try breathing as you do the small balancing exercises on the move. Downhill running or 'schussing' is one of the basic stances of

ski-ing, and it is important that you spend extra time practising it, so that you can instinctively adopt a comfortably balanced stance on the skis as soon as they start to slide.

Getting up from a fall

If you take a tumble while sliding down, there are two points to remember. Both skis must be lifted or shuffled round until they are side by side across the slope – as when you want to side step up the slope – and they must also be on the downhill side of your body. You are then ready to bend forward until your head is over your boots, when a quick push up with the hand or sticks from near to the body will have you standing upright again, without any great strenuous effort. If the skis insist on sliding away from you as you try to stand up, then they are not properly horizontal to the slope, or you are not leaning sufficiently forward to get your weight over the boots. In deep powder snow it is difficult to push off the loose snow; the snow rings on the poles can sink very deep as they take weight pressure. Then one way of spreading the pressure on the snow is to cross the ski poles flat in the snow, and push off with the hand at the crossing point. If your skis have released the bindings from the boots, then stamp out a step area in the snow before attempting to fix the skis back on.

Never be frightened of falling. Losing your balance and taking a spill is part of the process of learning to ski. Even experts take the odd fall now and then, especially if they, too, are learning or practicing a new development of ski technique. Once you begin to lose your balance, do not stiffen up and try to fight off the inevitable. Try to relax, and sit down to the side of skis so that you take the bump on your rear – it's the most well-cushioned part of your anatomy. Avoid stretching out the hand and fingers into the snow to arrest the fall. Instead, if possible lift the poles well out of the way, and keep the legs together.

31

1. Straight-running position

Correct way to fall-down!

Getting up from a fall

Figure 20.

Sliding through bumps and hollows

The ground over which you ski is not all smooth and level, and the snow on ski runs is soon made bumpy by turning and packing down the snow into bumps and grooves. Ski-ing over these undulations requires the skier to make compensating movements of the body and legs, so as to remain in a balanced control attitude. Your legs have to act like the shock absorbers on car wheels, compressing and extending over the undulations of the ground. The legs again do all the work and as the skis ride over a bump are folded under the body by bending the knees and ankles, stretching out again as the skis slide into the dip. The upper part of the body follows a less bumpy line as the legs iron out the dips, so that it is easier to stay in balance over the skis. Just standing up and making a small flex of the legs will only bounce you off the tops of the bumps, or pitch you forward into the upward sloping part of the bump. The idea is to stay over the skis as they quicken up and slide into the hollows. If the hollow is particularly deep, lean forward and stretch out the legs, then advance one ski in front of the other, so that you avoid being pitched forward off balance. Immediately the skis start to ride up the bump, fold the legs whilst leaning slightly back on the heels, if necessary, to compensate for the sudden rise of the skis under the body. Over the crest lean forward again ready to straighten the legs. It's just like riding the big dipper – rushing down into the valleys and slowing up on the humps. Find any ridge or hollow that will give you practice at this very necessary feeling of riding into and over bumpy ground, again with a runout on to level snow in order to slow down.

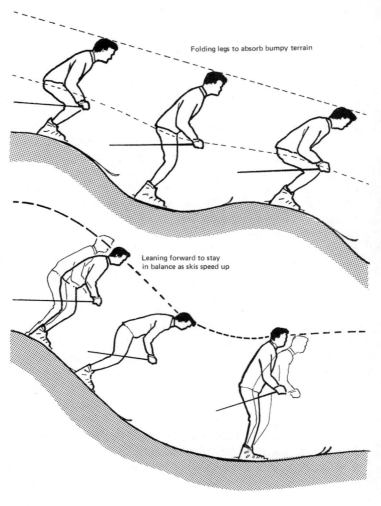

Folding legs to absorb bumpy terrain

Leaning forward to stay
in balance as skis speed up

Figure 21. Riding over bumps and hollows.

34

How to slow down and stop – the basic snowplough

Obviously you have to be able to apply the brakes to slow down once started on a slide downhill. Ski-ing consists of constantly avoiding hazards like trees, rocks and other obstacles, slowing down, turning and stopping if necessary. The most elementary way of doing this is by spreading the skis out in V form, so that you glide and brake off both inside ski edges. This is the snowplough. Just like a snowplough clearing snow from a road, the skis are spread out from the tips by opening the legs with the boots wide apart, so that you can push out the snow as they slide forward. Because your feet are apart it is a stable position to do at slow speeds, but is awkward to try at first and also tiring to hold for any long periods of ski-ing downhill. Choose a spot on

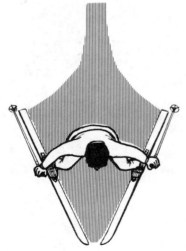

Figure 22. Snowplough position – spread of ski heels.

2. Snowplough position

the flat part of your nursery slope, stand with feet together then by flexing the legs to rise up on the skis, open out the heels with a quick push to slide them apart. Keep bending and stretching out the legs, so that you open out both skis at the same time, tilting the skis just a little on to the inner edges, and finishing in a pin-toed position. If you have trouble pushing the skis apart, give a little bounce of the heels to spread the feet open. Climb back up your slope, and step round to face downhill holding on to your poles as before. Now step the skis out into the snow-plough angle, press your knees forward along the line of the skis, not in towards one another. If you have the correct feeling of pressing on the inside of the feet down on to the inner ski edges, you should be able to stand in position when the poles are lifted out of the snow. If the skis begin to slide, the angle of the V is not wide enough, and you must press out both heels a little more. Stand with equal weight on both skis, and by leaning forward from the ankles and bringing the hips forward, the skis will slide. Try to feel just sufficient edge press to allow both skis to skid downhill without digging into the snow. The stance over the skis is exactly the same as a straight run, the poles held pointing behind out of the way, with the hands comfortably apart at waist level. The snowplough is a feeling that is strange to acquire at first, being unnatural to your normal movements, but it gives you the elementary control of braking by using the edges of the ski soles. If you have difficulty holding the legs apart in a relaxed manner, then look down before you start off the next time you are at the top of the slope, see if your knees are pushed forward towards the ski tips, and that you can press your ankles on the front of the boots. In this way you keep your weight pressure off the ski heels, and will find it much easier to hold the backs of the skis brushed apart.

There are several exercises that you can try while sliding down holding the snowplough. Bending and stretching the body and legs will make the angle of the skis either smaller or wider. Slide forward and stretch up slightly, the skis will glide a little quicker as the legs close towards one another and the skis have less plough angle. Bend the knees and ankles and sink down on the skis, and the backs of the skis will be spread out wider to slow the skis down. Practice this rising and sinking of the body over the skis, until you can brake to stop before reaching the bottom of the slope. Try starting with the skis parallel, pressing out into the plough angle to slow down, then rising up to let the skis come back together again, finally sinking down to slow and stop with the plough.

Figure 23. Snowplough glide and braking position.

The first turns using the Snowplough

Now that you have some kind of braking action you are ready to enjoy the fun of ski-ing that makes it such a great pleasure once you become proficient. Awkward though the snowplough is, at slow speeds it can be used to make you able to steer round in any direction you wish to go, providing that the slope is not too steep. If you have pressed down or edged more on one ski than the other while snowploughing straight down, you may have noticed that your skis have swerved across the slope. This is the principle of turning the skis at this stage: press down with more weight on one ski than the other. We do this by flexing the legs and pushing the knee down and forward more on one ski. This ski will then turn in the general direction to which it is pointing. Just a small press and push out of the ski heel will swerve your path downhill. Try this from a straight snowplough glide downhill with not too wide a plough angle. Pressing down and forward on the left ski and left leg will steer the skis across the slope to the right, and pressing on the right ski will steer over to the left. The golden rule to remember is that the ski to the outside of the turning path has to have the turning pressure applied to it. You can do these turns from the straight glide to turn and stop as you eventually begin to travel horizontally to the slope angle. Practise these turning stops both ways, then do rhythmic presses from one ski to the other, making small snaking, swerving paths down your slope. Eventually you can make the turns more precise and longer. As the skis steer across the slope and before they stop, stand up between the skis with your weight equally between them as the skis will begin to turn back downhill. By bending the leg and pressing on the opposite ski you will then be able to steer round back in the opposite direction. Linking these movements is called Snowplough Turning, and making a

39

Figure 24. Snowplough turning – pressing and steering the outer ski.

series of S turns down the slope means that you have really arrived as a skier. You are now ready to go up a little further on the nursery slope and to do longer controlled runs.

Ski-ing across the slope

Most of ski-ing is spent in crossing the slope before or while turning. This is called Traversing. To make the skis track across the slope, requires the basic sliding stance downhill to be modified in order to bite the ski edges into the snow, as you do when sidestepping uphill. To make the stance more comfortable, the upper ski is advanced slightly, so making the whole body face slightly diagonally to the line of the skis. Press both knees forward and then tilt the legs in towards the slope sufficiently to give a grip of the ski edges into the snow. It makes it much easier to hold the tracking line if more of the weight pressure is put on the lower ski's inner edge, leaning out the upper body over this ski to ensure that a good sliding balance is achieved. Again try these slides across the slope with the skis parallel, stop by stepping the skis one at a time up the slope, or press out the heels to snowplough and slow down.

Practical pointers

1. Ski with your feet slightly apart. Don't try to ski with your feet close together until you can ski proficiently.

2. Look forward. You should just be able to see your hands on the edge of your vision, don't look down at your boots and skis, you can't 'will' your skis round!

3. Cultivate being able to ski along on one ski at a time.

Figure 25. Stance over the skis for traversing across the slope.

4. Get the 'feel' of the snowplough first standing still on the flat.

5. Keep your ski poles always pointing behind you.

Common errors

WALKING – trying to lift the entire ski off the snow at each step. Slide the ski forward on the snow.

CLIMBING – not edging the skis correctly, trying to press on the snow with the ski flat. Not using the poles to push on as you step. Allowing the skis to slide backwards or forwards by moving them from a line across the slope.

STRAIGHT RUNNING – stiff and out of balance by bending upper body forward from the waist, with rigid ankles and legs. Arms stiff and reaching too far forward.

GETTING UP FROM A FALL – trying to push and get up by placing your hand or poles too far away from your body. Trying to get up from the downhill side of your skis. Move around so that your skis are across the slope on the lower side.

SNOWPLOUGH – not having the correct 'feel' of the legs spread apart stance. Having too stiff a posture, so that only one leg and ski glides in the snowplough angle, with the other ski digging its inner edge in too hard.

2 · Using the Training Ski Tow

The open gentle slopes prepared specially as a 'nursery area', in most ski resorts, are provided with some form of short uphill mechanical lift. These basic training areas are usually found immediately in the village or town where an easy gradient open slope is available, although sometimes these nursery training areas are located higher on the mountains above the resort, in order to ensure good snow conditions and to have a large easy slope. In this latter case, it will mean that you have to take some form of mountain transport to reach these slopes, but it is well worth the extra effort in order to learn on a specially prepared and groomed slope.

The trainer ski tow pulls you back up to the top of the slope at a very gentle pace, and all you have to do is to stand upright on your skis and slide on them back uphill. It is the same as ski-ing downhill with your skis parallel, except that the lift cable is the pulling force, and you do the guiding by keeping the skis pointing along the track in the snow.

Now that your skis are not too strange, you can save your energy and learn more quickly by using the trainer ski tow. By being able to practise and enjoy the basic ski-ing manoeuvres without having to climb back uphill, you will soon be ready to progress to the next learning stages.

How to use ski tows

Your first introduction to a ski tow is that of joining the lift queue or line. Slide or step along in turn, and avoid stepping or

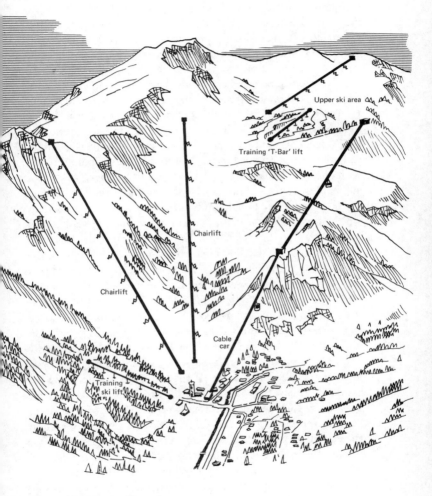

Figure 26. Ski area layout.

ski-ing over other people's skis and sticks. Have ready your lift ticket or cash to buy a ticket, before your turn to pass by the ticket office comes along. Then you won't have to rush and fumble for tickets at the last moment, which is very awkward, while at the same time you are holding ski poles and gloves.

All of the several types of ski tows have one thing in common, and that is they are designed to transport you uphill easily. However, there are certain things that you must know and obey in order to use them safely. Always step into the line of the tow or lift, facing the way it is going. Your skis will slide you uphill, so both must be stepped parallel on to the take-off point, in line with the tow track. Take your hands out of the pole straps, and hold both poles in the hand to the outside of the tow, leaving the other hand free to hold on to the tow-bar. The lift attendant will help you into position, and you must then be ready to be handed the tow-bar, placing it just below your seat. Ensuring that your skis are parallel, be immediately prepared to take the pull. On most tows the take-off is a slow smooth pull, but it is as well to be ready for any extra jerk that the type of lift may make. Once you are on the way uphill, all that is required is to stand there and flex your legs to take any ruts or bumps that may be in the track. Relax and let the tow do all the pulling work. Do not pull with your arm on to the bar as this is unnecessarily tiring; now is the time for having a chat with your partner or just looking at the passing scene. At the top there is a prepared flat area on the snow for you to get off the lift. Step one ski at a time away from the tow, at the same time letting go of the bar or obeying the instruction and diagram notices that are placed at the getting off point, clearly telling you the correct procedure for leaving the tow. As you slide away just keep a lookout for any tow-bars that may be hanging loose from the cable – it's no use cracking your head now that you have managed to reach the top. Should you start to slide backwards once you have reached the getting off point, spread your skis out in a V with the heels together, and use the Herringbone step to walk out of trouble.

If you do fall off the tow at any point, shuffle or crawl to the outside first before you try to get up, so that you are clear of the track and other skiers coming up behind you. Then when you are in a safe position you have plenty of time to fix your skis and find your goggles, hat, etc! This is particularly important at the top of a tow, where falling down on the exit area can block the path of all the other skiers getting off the lift.

Types of ski tows

One of the most common forms of ski tow is the 'T-Bar' tow. This consists, as its name implies, of a series of inverted wooden T towing bars fastened to the cable by a spring loaded recoil line. Two skiers are towed side by side, placing the T-Bar crosspiece under the behinds of the skiers. It helps with this type of tow to have a partner roughly the same height in order to have the pull taken equally. The attendant hands the bar between the two skiers, and it is up to you to hold the bar and ensure that it stays in position below your seat. Letting the bar slip too low by your knees, or high in the small of the back, will give you an uncomfortable ride. Many skiers, using a tow for the first time, think that they have to sit down on the bar, and they then fall-off as a result! All you have to do is stand up and be dragged along, stepping the skis to keep in the track – don't try and snowplough to steer the skis, you may cross your ski tips or put the back of your skis across your partner's.

Another form of popular tow is the 'Poma Lift' or Téléski, pulling one skier at a time by J shaped bars. The bars are not permanently fixed to the cable, and the attendant waits until you are in position before handing the bar to you, slipping the bar with its end plate between your legs so that it rests snugly at the

47

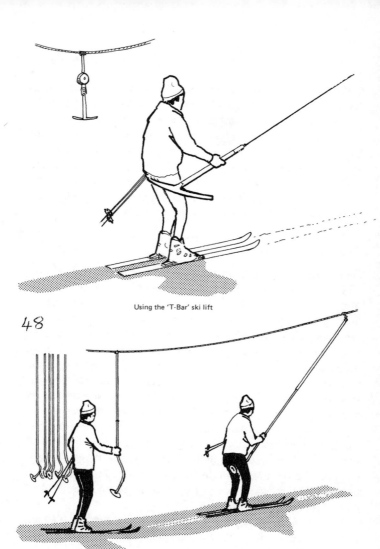

Using the 'T-Bar' ski lift

48

The Poma ski tow

Figure 27. Using ski tows.

back of the thighs. The bar is then automatically engaged with the main cable and you are on your way, sometimes with a sudden jerk, so always be prepared for instant lift-off with these tows! Riding the Poma Lift is exactly the same as a T-Bar. Stand erect and keep the knees flexed. Get off by pulling on the bar, opening your legs to slip out the bar and disc in front of you, then let go and step off to the side. The simplest form of ski tow, is the 'ropetow', where an endless rope is driven round a pulley at the top and bottom of the slope. Using a ropetow is not difficult. Simply maintaining a good grip on the rope is the most energetic part of riding the tow. It helps to have both hands free to hold on the rope, and the poles should be hung from the wrist of the outside hand. Step the skis into line and take hold of the rope, ready for the jerk as you tighten your grip on the rope. Lean back slightly and shuffle your skis forward to help the take-off. As with all tows, stand up and steer your skis to stay in the track. To ensure that any loose clothing does not become entangled with the rope, tuck anything hanging free well out of the way before moving up to take hold of the rope. Rope tows can cause heavy wear on expensive ski gloves, so if you are going to use a tow regularly it will pay to keep an old pair of gloves or suitably heavy duty gloves specially for this purpose.

Your first runs off the trainer tow

Once you have reached the top of the tow, and moved clear of the other skiers coming up on the lift, then take hold of the poles correctly and prepare yourself to move off. The long open slope may invite you to take a long straight swoop down to the bottom again. If you are that enthusiastic, then resist the temptation. Remember that you can pick up speed very quickly on skis, and the faster you ski the more difficult is any kind of controlling movement required to avoid hazards and obstacles. In addition there are plenty of learner skiers around who are just going through the same phase of getting used to controlling their skis. Speeding through these slower skiers is not only dangerous for collisions, but also discourteous and unnerving. There can also be nothing more humiliating than shouting for a clear passage and after taking the slope straight as a bullet, losing your balance half way down, and never arriving at the bottom – usually to cheers from the assembled gallery!

Edge your skis correctly, and traverse away from the lift across the slope. Now is the time to use these runs to practice the basic turning and controlling movements you have been trying out for the last hour or so down below on your own small slope. Let the skis run across the slope, just fast enough for you to remain in balance – about 6 to 8 mph as a guide. Turn back across the snow by opening both skis out into a snowplough. The lower ski will slide out easily but it may be necessary to push the upper ski heel against the slope to spread the skis open. Once you are gliding along with your weight pressure equal and both inner edges of the skis, the skis will start to turn themselves downhill. The turning or steering of the skis over the snow is made by pressing down and bending the knee and ankle forward over the ski to the outside of the turn, as you have tried before. This time you may be moving just a little faster. Then let the skis slide, as this makes turning easier, but if you are just a little tense about the speed, then open the skis out a little more at their heels to brake and slow down, until you feel relaxed and in complete control. One of the basic mistakes many learner skiers make in the early stages is to stiffen and lock up their muscles into the required attitude over the skis, performing the manoeuvre correctly, but not actually feeling the effect of edging or shifting of balance through their feet and legs. The body should be generally relaxed so that smooth flexing and bending of the legs and whole body make it less of an effort to apply the correct controlling technique. No muscle power is required to make the skis turn, since the feet and legs do all the work with your arms and poles held comfortably to the side for balance. However, as you are now going to ski further and longer than you have done previously, you will find that you become more relaxed as you become more familiar with the speed of the skis and can stand up in balance. You can now look around and search out a suitable line to take, since not all the snow is smooth and packed down flat. There are churned up patches, and bumps and hollows to negotiate, while there may be a rock or tree root sticking up that has to be avoided. Be on the look out all the while for the things to avoid and the best place to ski over or turn on. Not only down the slope on the snow ahead are there potential hazards, but you should remember that other skiers may be coming down behind you. Therefore, before changing your direction, a quick glance uphill to see if you are not going to ski into the path of someone else is one of the basic rules of the Skiers Code that is important for your own safety.

Once you have worked out a rough line down the slope, try longer turns, making smooth sweeps across the snow rather than trying to get the skis round too quickly. On a longer turn you have more time to think and feel the movements required, holding the pressure on the outer turning ski to control the steering by the inside working edge of the ski until you have started to traverse back across the slope. If it helps, lean out sideways just a little from the waist, to apply more turning pressure to the working ski. Do not twist the upper body round either in towards the turn or facing out, but try to remain fairly square to the skis and the direction you wish to go. Pick a traversing line across a series of bumps if you can find any on the slope – anything to test your balance and feel what happens to the skis when you go over any changes in the smoothness or angle of the slope. Flex your knees and ankles as the skis go over the bump and straighten up as they slide down in the hollows. If you start to slow up as the skis ride up on a bump, place both poles into the snow and give a push to keep on moving.

These first runs are going to give you memories for a lifetime. The thrill of sliding without effort is an excitement that cannot be adequately described. If you are enjoying the release at being able to accomplish something new, then this is the right frame of mind to learn and progress further. Tiredness or trying to ski too recklessly may only find you becoming frustrated at attempting to turn properly, or even injuring yourself.

Having taken several runs using long traverses and wider turns, the last few go's on the lift should see you attempting to link several turns together in succession. Picking a continuous smooth part straight downhill, hold the snowplough glide with skis apart, and by using more pronounced and flowing leg and body movements, turn the skis from side to side without traversing in between. From a downpress on one ski – if you are turning to the right, then the left ski and leg will do the work – straighten up to give equal weight to both skis and allow them to return downhill, where you can then press down and turn the opposite ski and leg. All that follows is a smooth series of movements, which is the secret of making ski-ing easy to perform.

You can also make your runs more varied by looking for rounded bumps on the snow. These help you to turn the skis and, as you will find out later, are very much part of ski-ing down prepared trails. Ski up towards the bump and open out both skis into the plough angle as you ride up towards the high point of the snow. Let the skis start to slide around the crest, then bend the ankle and knee forward on to the turning ski, to steer the skis round the curved shape of the bump. If you do it correctly the skis will almost turn themselves round and back across the slope. You may also find that instead of the inside ski remaining spread out in the plough angle, it will start to slide in

52

Figure 28. Snowplough turn round a bump on the slope.

parallel with the outer turning ski. Try and allow this inner ski to skid into a slightly forward or advanced position as the turn is finishing, so that you are already prepared to traverse comfortably across the snow.

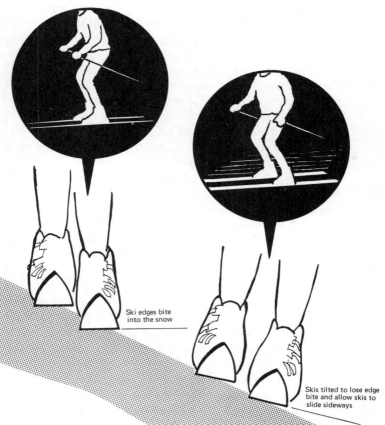

Ski edges bite into the snow

Skis tilted to lose edge bite and allow skis to slide sideways

Figure 29. Side slipping.

If the bump is sufficiently large to make a fairly large rounded turn, try to close the inside ski earlier, by smoothly narrowing the plough angle. This is not difficult to do if you are putting most of the turning weight pressure on the outer ski. As the skis close together, a sideways skid down the slope may result as the skis momentarily flatten off their edge bite. This is called 'side-slipping', and is another important part in the process of learning to ski eventually with the skis parallel all the time. You can get the feel of making the skis side-slip by picking a part of the slope that is not too shallow, and by placing both poles on the uphill side of the skis which are positioned horizontally on the snow, pushing downhill sideways with a sinking movement of the legs to skid both skis. Side-slipping is only effected by the feet and legs. Lower the whole body slightly over the skis and press the knees away from the slope. Then the tilt of the skis into the snow is lessened, until there is no hold on the edges. As the skis start to skid, you must go with them, leaning outwards sufficiently to stay in balance without leaning back or too far forwards. It is a very small movement that requires careful feel and just enough confidence to lose a grip on the snow into the sideways drift. After trying to side-slip the skis from a static position, traverse across the slope and make small nibbles at losing the edge bite of both skis. Then, sinking down and pressing both knees away from the slope, allow an induced skid to take place. Your natural reactions will stop the skid from going too far by pressing the knees back in to the uphill side to tilt the skis back on to their edges. This is just another exercise at this stage but you will find later how valuable side-slipping is in the whole enjoyment of longer ski runs. Don't forget to try skidding on both sides, if the slope is steep enough. Then allow longer slips until you can control the movement, perhaps with your feet apart to give you a wider base to stay in balance. Before you leave the trainer tow slope, you should practice being able

4. Side slipping

to stop or take quick avoiding action – that is if you have not already had to do so! Make quick snowplough stops straight downhill, or stop by making a sharp turn in towards the slope. It may be nice to enjoy the bliss of creaming down now that you have your ski legs, but you must be ready to take emergency action at any time. As soon as you feel tired, stop! – Go and have a drink on the balcony of a café or restaurant near the run, and look at the other skiers. Ski-ing is a visual artform and you can learn much by watching good skiers perform their prowess at the sport, even though the most elegant and experienced can suddenly end up in an inglorious heap!

Why learn the snowplough and traverse?

You may ask why learn the snowplough, in particular, when ultimately the goal to be reached is to ski with your feet parallel! There are many arguments in favour of teaching an all-parallel system, but it is a practical fact that for slow controlled manoeuvrability at the initial learning stage, the snowplough still plays a very important role. However, with the use of the shorter skis, and the ever increasing use of an even shorter ski programme, there is less tendency to remain at the stage of snowploughing longer than is necessary. Some skiers find their ski legs quicker than others who may be just that much more timid at experimenting with different skidding exercises.

The snowplough is an awkward position to hold, since we do not normally walk around with our feet wide apart! It will find muscles along the inside of your leg and thigh that you never knew existed, and this is where doing a series of pre-conditioning exercises helps to avoid becoming stiffened up after only one day on skis. But at least the snowplough provides a foundation of being able to turn, brake and stop, making you able to manoeuvre yourself down the easier gradient runs, within a short time of first putting skis on. With the skis in the V shape, either ski is already pointing to turn in that direction, positioned for being steered as you may require on your run downhill. At the same time it is giving you valuable edge control feel on the skis, and you will soon sense how little you have to edge the ski over on its running surface before it bites into the snow to slow you down. Alternatively, by flattening the ski, the edge bite is lessened and the skis are allowed to drift and glide sideways. The feel of what happens when you tilt the skis over from edge to flat sole is the mechanics of ski sliding control, just like the brakes and steering of a car.

Traversing is the means by which you check your speed downhill. Almost half of the time spent in ski-ing down a slope is spent in some line of diagonal traverse across the slope. It is the basic position from which all ski manoeuvres are made, and is therefore important for learning the more advanced ski-ing turns.

Practical pointers

1. Working edge of the ski – feel that you are using the inside edge of the ski that is doing all the work when turning or traversing.

2. Ankle and knee bend – concentrate on maintaining a good bend in these leg joints when you want to brake, steer or stop the skis.

3. Press on the right ski to go left, press on the left ski to go right.

4. Keep the ski tips close together when snowploughing. It keeps the effective angle you require to brake with the skis down to the minimum spread of the legs.

5. Lean back but don't sit down on ski tows.

Common errors

SNOWPLOUGH TURNS – flattening the ski that is doing the turning work, by letting the boot and knee roll outwards, instead of steering the ski on its inside working edge.

SNOWPLOUGH TURNS – straightening the turning leg and twisting the upper body round to face inside the turn, again causing a flattening of the ski and losing the steered control.

TOO STIFF BALANCE POSTURE – bending forward from the waist with stiff legs, losing a relaxed stance over the skis.

TRAVERSING – not sufficiently advancing the uphill ski so that it is allowed to drag behind and cause tracking difficulty on both skis.

LEANING INTO THE SLOPE – instead of standing upright to press down on the skis, the upper body leans into the slope, especially if the gradient steepens off, and the skis are pushed away from under you.

3 · On Easy Ski Runs

Now that you are independently mobile, the easy ski runs that run down the mountains of most ski resorts are instantly opened up as a challenge and enjoyment for you. Have a careful look at the ski runs diagram or map of your particular resort, and you find it is not too difficult to pick out a run that will suit your first real ski downhill. In Alpine countries the markings for an easy piste are by yellow or blue lines and marker posts. In North American ski areas they are indicated by green square markers. If you are in doubt, ask around for the easy run down. There are always plenty of skiers about to offer advice as to the merits of various ski pistes or runs. Indeed you may find offers to guide you down, since ski-ing has this great camaraderie that makes it such a unique sport.

The mechanical uplift may take the form of a chairlift to take you up to the starting point of your run, and as with ski tows it is useful to know just a little of the correct way to use them.

Using chairlifts

There are several different kinds of chairlifts. Some are single chairs, others are double and even triple-seater chairs. While most lifts have the chairs permanently fixed to the cable, there are some that mechanically clip the chairs on and off the cable. The latter are very simple to use, as the chair is stationary when you get on and off, so it is just a matter of walking to and from the chair. It is when you use the fixed chair while still wearing your skis that some pre-knowledge of the procedure is useful.

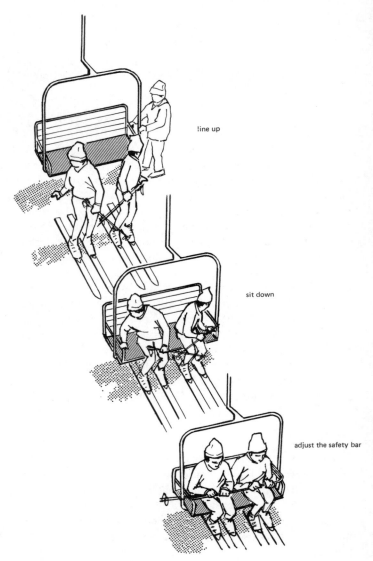

line up

sit down

adjust the safety bar

Figure 30. Using chairlifts.

62

The lift queue or line is similar to that of the ski tow, stepping in order up to the take-off point. Make sure that your skis are parallel and pointing up the line of the lift. Hold both poles in the hand to the outside of the lift. Move your lunchbag or rucksack round to your front, so that you can sit back in the chair. Turn your shoulders round to look for the approach of the chair, and as it moves forward sit down in it as soon as it touches the back of your legs. With your free hand you can take hold of the side or hanging tube just to steady yourself while you sit more comfortably on the chair. On some lifts you may slide along for a short distance with your skis still on the snow. Then make sure that they stay parallel until clear of the ground. Once you are underway, swing across the safety bar and step for your skis, and see that you don't drop your poles or gloves off the chair – it's a long way back to fetch them! Keep your eyes open for the signs on the lift pylons that tell you the correct way to get off the chair. As you approach the top, open up the safety bar and keep your ski tips up so that they do not catch on the unloading platform. When your skis touch down, then move forward on the chair until you can stand up on the skis and slide off under your own steam. The exit ramp down which you slide is usually straight ahead so that as you stand up and ski off, the chair is immediately well clear of your head. On some lifts however, it is necessary to step to the side and walk away from the chair; the attendant at the top will swing the chair out of your way as you step off it. To use a double chairlift is exactly the same, holding the poles to the outside, and getting off on your own track or according to the directions of the lift. As with all lifts, once you are off the chair, move well clear of the unloading area to allow others to get off. A final tip is that of just doing a few leg bending, squatting and stretching exercises before you take off, especially if it has been a cold ride up on the chair. Frozen muscles are not conducive to good ski control.

First time down a mountain ski run

Now that you have completed your first stages of learning the basics of ski technique – walking, climbing, and linking snow-plough turns – you are ready to build up towards more advanced ski-ing. The most controlled, enjoyable and graceful way to ski is with your legs and skis together and parallel to one another. This way it is less tiring to control the skis, and as a result requires not so much effort once the feeling has been acquired. On your run down now, the next stage is to have a go at skidded turns by swinging the skis round and across the slope parallel to one another, rather than holding too long in a stemmed out position.

The first impression that you may get of the ski run, having moved away from the top of the lift, is that the piste or trail is much more confined in width than down on the training slopes. The run may be flanked with trees, or may be a prepared piste out of the untracked snow on either side. Take the first part steadily, in order to get your bearings, and become familiar with the amount of space on the run that you have in which to manoeuvre. Remember always to keep your ears and eyes open for other skiers who may be coming by faster than yourself. How to collide with other skiers is not part of the learning progression!

Instead of being all nicely smoothed out with just gentle undulations, as on the nursery slope, all ski runs become shaped into a series of bumps and hollows. The steeper the slope, the larger these humps, being formed by the passage of many pairs of skis – skidding, scraping and scouring the snow into rounded lumps called 'moguls'. Every ski run has them in a lesser or greater form, and although special snow-tracked machines can groom the snow back smooth, moguls can quickly form again when skiers run down in any numbers. These bumps should not be regarded as horrible obstacles, but more as a challenge to make ski-ing interesting, and above all as a help in learning to turn. Ski down the first part of the run as you have done before, traversing where the run goes sideways across the mountain and linking your snowplough turns with more rhythmic sinking and rising body movements. Where there is a bend in the run, take the longer way round on the outside edge where the bumps are always smaller in size and there will be more loose snow lying about on which you can get the skis to grip. If you are just a little shy of the slope, perhaps being up on this huge mountain puts you on the defensive, or looking down into the valley may make you feel a little concerned about getting down in one piece! Try to breathe normally – some people suddenly hold their breath when they become apprehensive of the slope downhill. Concentrate on the job in hand, look at the snow just in front of you and relax any stiffening of legs and arms. Don't lean into the slope as this will tend to push the skis away from underneath you. If anything, tilt your upper body to the outside so that you can get your body over the lower 'working' ski.

By letting your skis run just a little faster, you will find that your skis want to slide parallel, rather than spread apart in the plough. Pick the next open area on the run that comes along, to begin practising 'plough swings'.

The plough swing and basic swing turn

From a line going down and across the slope, open the skis out into a snowplough and allow the skis to turn downhill. By making a definite downsink movement on to the outer ski, the inner ski can be slid into a parallel position, rolling the ski and foot over to change the sliding pressure from inner to outside edge. The result will be to make a swing out and back in towards the slope,

65

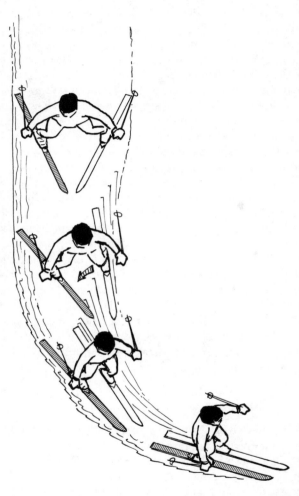

Figure 31. Closing the skis into a parallel swing from the snowplough.

with the skis in an open parallel skidded arc. The important part of this swing manoeuvre is that the inside ski is physically turned by the foot, helped by the fact that the ski should have only a small amount of weight pressure on it. As the skis skid parallel, the skier keeps both knees pressed forward in the direction of the turn, holding this position with the inner ski slightly in advance, until both skis can be opened out in a plough and the swing tried again. If you freeze up into the plough stance, then give a series of leg flexes to press on the turning skis, gradually giving small bouncing presses to close the inner ski. Avoid making the mistake of lifting and stamping the ski in parallel. Then you would lose the smooth turning action of swinging the skis together.

Practice this movement of closing the skis into a parallel swing as a series of rhythmic movements. You can do this quite easily without losing too much height by making full turns. Open the skis and start to turn downhill followed by the down-sink back onto the lower ski, swinging both skis together with the closing action of the inner. Immediately open the skis out to plough turn downhill followed by downsink and parallel swing back across the slope. This series of half-turns are called garland swings, and give a continuous feeling of turning and coupled closing of the inner ski into the swings, as a repetitive action. You should do at least half a dozen of these garlands, before turning fully to ski back and try the exercise from the other side.

The basic swing turn uses the extra tempo in ski-ing speed that you have now acquired to make longer radius turns, finishing the turn with a longer parallel skid than before. Traverse over the snow with the feet slightly apart, then open the skis into a narrow stemmed glide—about half the spread of your normal snowplough angle. Stand up on both skis and allow them to turn downhill, letting them speed up just a little

more. Close the inner ski into the outer by a smooth but positive downsink of the legs, pressing more on the ski to the outside of the turn as usual. By pushing the knees forward into the direction you wish to steer, both skis will skid in a long swing out of the turn. Finish by traversing with the skis parallel, but slightly apart–remember the upper ski is kept advanced by about 4 in. to make it comfortable to stand over the skis on the slope, and also prevents the tips becoming crossed.

Using the short ski will enable you to close the skis into the parallel swing without any great difficulty. It may take several turns down the run to begin to feel that you have to turn and skid the ski from gliding on the inside of your foot to the outside edge, pushing the ski slightly forward as you do so. You will notice that the emphasis is on the controlling of the skis only by the legs, and that the upper body is not twisted into unnatural static positions that confuse the learner and detract from the importance that feet and legs play in turning the skis. If you still find it hard to shift over and glide on the outer ski while closing the inner – and also for those skiers learning on standard length skis – then a gentle bounce of the ski heels by flexing the legs sharply will help to bring the skis together.

Take the rest of the run practising these swings, when you can also try placing or planting the ski pole on the inside of the turn to help the start of the swing. If there are steep bends on the run and it is not possible to take the outer curve, then side-slip down the steeper pitches. Pick out the largest bumps or ridges and ski up on the crest, then simply drift down with the tips and heels just off the snow – there is always a flat spot of loose snow for you to stop on, even on the steepest slopes! Trying to side-slip down the hollow grooves between the bumps will flip the skis all over the place, even though it looks a better place down which to lose height. The tips and heels will catch in the curved sides of the groove, making it difficult for you to

69

5. Basic swing

put all your weight pressure on the centre of the skis under your boots, where it should be! Sink down on to the skis, moving both knees out from the slope just enough for the skis to tilt off their edges and drift downhill. Stay facing outwards once underway, looking for a place to stop or slow down, pressing your legs back into the slope to make the edges bite again. Where it is not possible to ski round on the easier gradient of the bed – usually there are steep banks of snow that prevent you from traversing anymore – it is always the best policy to side-slip down the first opportunity that comes along. Staying high on a traverse will only make it more difficult to find a suitable place to get out of trouble.

The skating step

At the bottom of the run, the slope flattens out and if you haven't sufficient speed to ski down back to the lift without vigorous use of the poles, then the use of the skating step will keep you gliding along.

To do the skating step, slide along on one ski lifting the other ski off the snow. Then step the lifted ski tip out to the side, and with a quick push off slide on to this ski at an angle to which you are facing. Lift up the other ski ready to step and glide forward at an angle on the other side. Step, lift and slide from side to side is the sequence of movements, coupled with the use of both poles planted to give a good push off. As well as a means of keeping you going where the terrain is flattish, the skating step can be useful for getting you out of trouble, such as when the skis become fixed into 'tramline' grooves in the snow, or if you ski into heavy snow where the skis will not turn.

Into the basic parallel turns

So far all your turns have been made by spreading open the

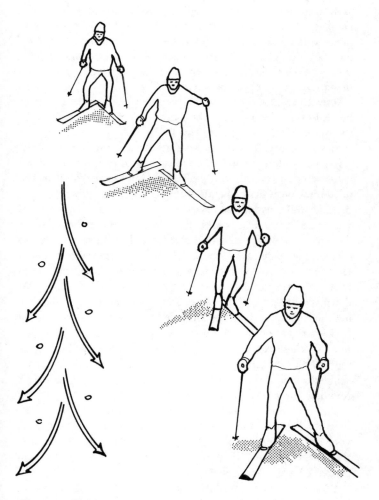

Figure 32. Skating step.

skis, and using a shift of weight pressure to steer the skis. Having practised doing the finishing half of turns with the skis parallel, the task now to learn is that of having both feet work together throughout the turn. This requires a little more careful timing of the movements involved so that both legs work as one to start and control the parallel skidding.

As with all new ski-ing technique movements, it is more than helpful to try the motions while stationary. Having returned to the top of the lift, move off and find a spot on the snow, well towards the edge of the run so that you are out of the way of skiers going down. Plant both poles well in front of you about a metre apart. Stand with your skis pointing downhill in the open track position. From an upright stance, sink down quickly, bending and twisting the knees to one side so that the ski heels are turned or fanned across the snow, flattening the skis just enough to allow them to skid sideways. Try the same exercise to the other side, using the quick drop to crank the legs and fan the ski heels over the snow, holding onto the poles to help take your weight. Pick a not too steep part of the slope, ski down straight and do the same motion, downsinking and twisting the legs by pushing the knees into the slope to skid both ski heels in an arc or swing in towards the slope to stop. Again you must do these parallel swings to either side, feeling the flattening of the skis to turn and the gradual edging of the skis as they are skidded round. Have a search round on the slope to find a large rounded hump or ridge around which to swing the skis.

You will need to get up a little more speed, then try and twist both knees and feet across the slope at right angles to your straight run. As well as turning the skis in a curving arc, this is also the way to stop by pushing the skis sideways and pressing both edges into the snow.

Parallel ski-ing is the start of the freedom to ski on any slope, in an elegant and effortless manner. The pleasures of ski-ing

Figure 33. Swing across the slope, from straight down the fall-line.

have only just started at this stage, and even if you never become absolutely proficient, the challenge is a constant stimulus to perfect your version of parallel turns. If you find that your progress so far has been satisfactory, then you are well on the way to try all the other exciting forms of advanced ski-ing manoeuvres.

Before you attempt to make the basic parallel turn, stop and look at the other skiers. Analyse simply how they turn their skis in a series of smooth, fluent parallel swings. It may be difficult to pick out small subtle movements, but the general rhythmic flow of the skiers' motions are easy to follow. Look how they use the terrain, and are able to make short or long turns at will. Once you have an idea of the technique required, and have done your practice exercises, try to follow behind someone who will ski at your speed. Imitating the movements of the person immediately in front is the quickest way to break into the habit of ski-ing parallel.

In the parallel swing the edges of both skis are released sufficiently to allow them to flatten, then skidded and swung round sideways in the turn until they are re-edged on their opposite sides to take up a new traverse line. The critical phase in the turn is at the start, triggering off the release of both skis into a simultaneous turning action. Once the turn is underway there is virtually no effort required, apart from controlling where you want to direct the skis.

We can do these starting movements in garland form, as before with the basic swing, across the slope. Traverse over the snow, make a small flex, press with both legs down on the skis, then rise up slightly forward to flatten the skis and swivel the front of the skis downhill. Don't let the skis turn too far, but sink down smoothly back over the lower ski to reapply the edges and steer the skis back on their traverse line. This exercise again requires a smooth follow-through of the movements, in

Figure 34. Parallel turn – starting exercise garland swing.

order to get the correct feel of starting the skis to turn, and both feet working as one.

The final form of the turn, using the wide track stance over the skis, is started just as in the garland exercise. Flex the legs, a small press of knees and ankles, followed by a straightening of the whole body to flatten both skis and turn the fronts downhill. As soon as the skis are starting to turn, then begin to apply more weight pressure to the outside ski of the swing. At the same time press both knees forward along the skis in a down-sink or half-kneeling motion to control the skidding of the swing. You should be already fairly familiar with the way in which to use the edges of the skis as you finish the turn. The upper body remains throughout the manoeuvre fairly square over the skis, facing always slightly towards the downhill side, and follows the advancing of the inside ski as the turn is made. You will have to try these turns successfully in a long run down, before a correct timing and feeling of both skis moving together is achieved. A speed of at least 8 m.p.h. will be needed for you to get this feeling, so do not be timid at letting the skis slide that bit extra.

Use of the pole plant in turning

One thing you will have noticed as you watch the other skiers going down is that they all seem to flick out their poles into the snow as they ski over it, in time with the dance of turning the skis from side to side. This use of the pole in turning plays a very important part in modern parallel ski-ing. Planting the pole on the inside of your turn helps to start the turning action, because it provides a pivot or aid to changing your weight from one ski to the other. On steeper slopes you may have to push really hard on the pole, as against rounded turns on easier gradients when the pole will only be used as a timing marker.

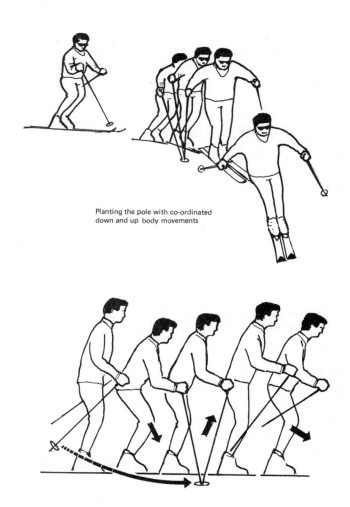

Planting the pole with co-ordinated
down and up body movements

Figure 35. Pole plant sequence.

Find a flat spot on the snow, and with your feet parallel but apart, give a gentle hop of the ski heels, leaving the tips on the snow. Now hop again, but this time hop the heels from side to side, pivoting from the tips as if they were nailed down into the snow. The springing action is in the legs, bouncing from the balls of the feet, letting the legs sink a little more as you land to the side, rather than a stiff, jarring landing. The pole action is made by swinging the hand forward to place the pole point roughly half way between the ski tip and the boot, at about 12 in. (30 cm) away from the side of the ski. The arm is swung forward with the hand and wrist turning to bring the pole forward, ready to be planted in the snow. Maintain the same grip on the pole handle the whole time, and don't allow the handle to swivel round in the palm by releasing your grip. Correct timing in using the pole plant with leg movement is crucial to making effortless parallel swings, especially in rapid succession of linked turns.

We can now couple the pole plant with the ski heel hops. Swing the pole on the left side and plant it with a downsink of the legs, now hop up and push off the pole to bounce the heels to the righthand side, landing with a cushioning sink of the legs. Lift the left pole out of the snow, and swing the right arm and pole forward to plant it in the snow, again with a downsink motion to give a little spring up of the heels, fanning them across the opposite lefthand side. Practice these movements to co-ordinate the sequence of pole-plant-hop to opposite side-down-sink, as an alternating bounce from right to left, giving a little press off the pole each time you displace the heels to the other side. Once you have the feel of this action, then you can give a press off the inside ski edges as you hop and land. You will have to press with more weight on the outer skis as you turn, so try to hop and land from right to left ski inner edges while moving both skis.

78

6. *Pole-plant parallel turn*

Ski down and find a reasonably open slope, then try these hops with pole plant while traversing across the snow. The hand and pole on the downhill side is planted with a flex of the legs just to bounce the ski heels, turn round and do the same in the opposite direction. Now you try planting the pole and hopping both heels uphill – away from the pole plant – to turn the skis downhill. If you give a smooth bounce followed by the cushioning downsink on to the skis, and remember to change your weight pressure on to the outer ski, the skis will go at once into parallel skid. This is your first wide track parallel turn. Correct co-ordination of down onto the pole plant followed by an immediate straightening or flexing of the legs to turn the skis to initiate the turn is the secret. The controlling arc of the swing is just the same as you have practiced before.

You should now look round at the terrain, searching for favourable spots to try your turns on. Nice rounded humps are the best. Ski up towards them and as you approach the crest or rounded top, sinkdown on to your pole plant. Straighten up and push off the pole, turning the skis by swivelling the tips or making a slight hop of the heels to the uphill side. Transfer your weight to the outer ski, at the same time sinking down by pressing the knees forward along the skis to steer them round the downhill side of the hump.

How to turn on the 'moguls' of your ski run

As said before, 'moguls' are there to be used, not shied away from as monsters to be avoided. Once you have the confidence to ski over and round them you will find that they are a source of additional ski-ing fun.

If you are still making basic swing turns, or cannot avoid stemming out the skis to start the turn, the way to use the mogul is to stem out the skis as you come up to the crest. Fold

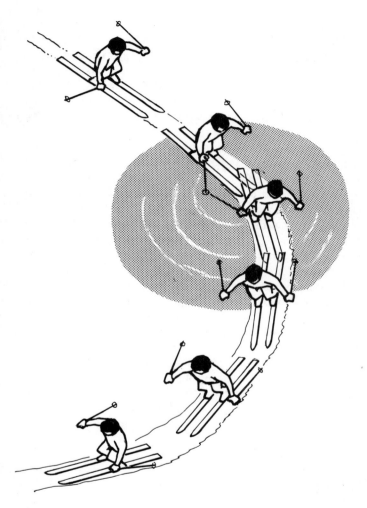

Figure 36. Parallel turn using a bump.

the legs a little more, then press both knees in the direction you wish to turn. You can also put the pole into the snow on the downhill side to aid turning. You will have to kneel forward on the skis as they start to slide down the steeper rounded side of the bump, but in the process they will close easily together – if necessary straighten or stretch out the legs into the hollow part of the mogul formation. Once the skis have steered round back across the line of descent, you can traverse and find the next bump to skid round. Sometimes there are a series of very sharp-sided bumps, usually on bends or steep pitches on the run. Traversing directly across the line of these bumps is awkward. Your tips are liable to hook up into the sides, as well as give you a real switchback ride. Step out of the way and avoid taking a line that is going to take you through the worst of these moguls, if you do not fancy turning at this particular point. However it may be best to sideslip out of the way, choosing the easier spot to drift down and away the deep grooves.

With the parallel turn, the sequence of turning is just the same, except that after planting the pole there may be no need to straighten or extend the body and legs to start the skis turning. As the skis come up on the mogul crest, both tips and heels will have less pressure on them, and the whole ski can be swivelled round off the planted pole. The knees press and steer the skis down and round the bump. Again, if the hollow is deep you will have to straighten out the legs to keep the skis in contact with the snow and maintain edge control to steer the skis towards the next bump.

Towards more rhythmic movements in turning

The long gentle gradient of the runout to your easy ski piste gives an excellent opportunity to have a go at linking small parallel turns. Ski-ing straight down the line of descent, or

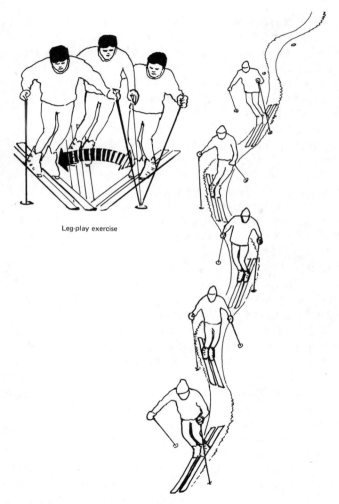

Leg-play exercise

Figure 37. Wedeln turns on easy slope.

83

fall-line, making these continuous snake-like turns is called *Wedeln* (German for waggle) and is a universal term in ski language for this performance of rapid successive wiggles of the skis. To do it correctly and fluently requires just the same pole plant and ski turning movements as were learned in the basic open parallel swing, but with a more relaxed, supple linking of the movements.

With the skis open, point them directly downhill, and dip slightly as you plant the pole on one side of your skis. Push off the pole and straighten up to lighten the skis for a fraction, while you turn your feet – pushing the ski heels and swivelling the fronts whilst sinking down smoothly on to the outside ski. The opposite arm is then brought forward to plant the pole to coincide with the sinkdown from the first turn. This then becomes the dip on to the pole with push off and rise up to turn both skis back in the opposite direction. The hands stay well to the front ready to synchronise the pole plant with the leg turning movements, until they flow in unison to control the rhythmic tempo of the turns. There will be a tendency to push the ski heels too far across the slope, braking on the edges, and allowing the skis to turn too much in an arc. If you stay facing downhill, keeping your hands and poles ready, the motions required to fan the skis from side to side do not demand strong forceful actions, but rather supple play of the legs from the hips. If any hazard suddenly crops up in front of you, the remedy is to sink down on one of the turns still further and steer the skis round a full turn, to slow down or avoid the obstacle. To get the feeling of rhythm, count your poleplants out loud, or sing to yourself – ski-ing with music will do wonders for your style!

Over these first learning stages in your progress into the realms of parallel ski-ing – the goal of a basic school technique – you may either have picked up the ability quickly, or have taken some time to eventually get the feeling. Having good reflexes, to check your balance and co-ordinate your controlling ski-ing movements, may see you progress into *Wedeln*-type turns in three days, providing you are in good shape physically and have ideal snow conditions. Otherwise you should have no great problems, like the majority of recreational skiers, of being able to perform rough parallel-type turns at the end of your first week. Vary your runs down, making use of all the easy pistes at your particular resort to give you a variety of different runs, each with their own special characteristics to test your newly acquired skills.

If you want to stop to take a rest while ski-ing down, or you take a fall and have to put your skis back on, the safest place to stand and do this is on the edge of the run. This is particularly important if the ski piste is not very wide. You don't want to be skied into by other skiers coming down and they may not see you until it's too late. So move off to the side where you can stand in safety, and don't forget before you decide to start off downhill again – just take a quick look uphill to see that it is clear for you to ski out onto the slope.

Having managed to turn proficiently to both left and right on medium packed slopes is just the introduction to this sport. There is a lot more to be learned about ski-ing faster, handling snow conditions, and different terrain, but the technique you now have is the key to moving into the great ski-ing world.

Why learn the parallel swing?

With the skis held parallel throughout your ski-ing manoeuvres, you have both edges of the skis to brake and use for steering control. It is safer, more natural, and less tiring to ski when both skis are tracking in the same direction. With the parallel turn you can ski for longer periods and at a higher speed. You can hold your skis apart in the open stance for stabilising your balance until you feel confident to bring your skis close together.

Practical pointers

1. Close the skis into the parallel skid by sinking down into the strong ankle and knee bend, then pressing both knees in the direction you wish to go.

2. Always face towards the downhill side when sideslipping, and keep the upper ski advanced.

3. Only the legs do the turning and steering action of the skis, and not your head and shoulders.

4. Advance your inside ski once you have started skidding the skis in a parallel swing.

5. Use the pole as an aid to turning; don't swing it too far forward near the ski tip.

Common errors

Closing the skis from the plough to parallel swing – difficult if you do not put more weight pressure on the outside ski, and use a downsink movement of the legs, to slide the skis parallel smoothly.

Stepping or stamping the ski into the parallel position from the snowplough.

Starting the parallel swing by moving the hips outwards as the skis are closed. The hips are held in the same relative position as the skis, inside hip and inside ski slightly more in advance.

Pole plant – not timing the downsink motion of the legs at the time of the pole being planted into the snow.

Trying to start the parallel turn by making the up-extending movement of the legs and body on the heels, and not in an up-forward motion, resulting in no start to the turn.

4 · Ski-ing from the Top of the Mountain

A trip to the top of the mountain does not necessarily entail being precariously perched on a forbiddingly steep peak, where only eagles fly, and only the expert skiers can flit down the walls of snow. Blue runs often enough, sneak off round easy shelves and shoulders that form the folds of the mountainside. If the ski resort is catering for the modern requirements of the holiday skier, then carefully prepared pistes will have been made to ensure that you, at your stage of ski-ing ability, can enjoy ski-ing off the mountain top.

The last form of uphill transport that we have to use is the Cable Car, or Gondola lift. These enclosed cabins carry skiers who are not wearing their skis, and time is taken up waiting to get in and making sure that your skis are securely fastened together. In the larger cabins several skiers, up to a hundred in the very big cars, stand together – loading and unloading from them while they are stationary. Gondolas take two or more skiers sitting down in comfort, with their skis placed in racks on the outside of the cabin. The only danger that you may come across is someone dropping his skis on you as he gets fed up with waiting in the queue, but some stations have installed continuous ski films in their waiting rooms to counter-act any boredom that may set in with their customers! Probably the best training for using cable cars at busy periods is to be had from being a commuter on the Underground!

Into more advanced parallel ski-ing

Until a few years ago, advanced ski-ing referred to those skiers who could do a fancy version of the basic parallel turn, and that was more or less the extent of the finer forms of technique. Now advanced ski-ing is the term covering a whole repertoire of different kinds of parallel and other high performance turns.

When you can make fluent controlled parallel turns, the whole terrain of a ski mountain becomes your playground. Every ski run is there for you to try, not necessarily recklessly like an olympic racer, but with enough control for you to enjoy the runs with confidence, and as a safe skier too!

No longer will ski-ing be just a matter of getting down a run or piste. You will now be able to 'do your own thing', seeking out the best snow or hunting for a group of moguls where you can freak out in gay abandon! The development of advanced ski turns owes much to the new techniques used in ski racing. These are adapted from those used by the racer who wants maximum controlled speed, to the needs of the recreational skier who is not so much concerned with speed, but wants to be able to ski down most slopes without losing control. The exploration into the refining and creating of advanced ski turns has now got to a stage where it is a complete subject in itself. Starting in the Advanced Ski School is like joining the Basic Ski School at the walking stage!

However, your ski lessons now take you on to practical use of the basic parallel turn, so that you can widen your enjoyment of ski-ing. If you are still using the shorter size of ski you should now graduate to a bit longer ski size. Otherwise your 175 cm ski length is still recommended, unless you really feel that a ski 10 or 20 cm longer will give you more edge tracking. Don't be talked into too long a ski – the more out front and

88

back the harder they are to turn, and the more likely they are to snag up in the moguls!

The parallel swing – finished form

The basic parallel turn, as tried in the previous chapter, uses an open ski stance to give you a broad balance platform to work on, but once you can perform these wide-track parallels the next stage is to refine the whole turn. Firstly, you must close your skis a little nearer to one another, not locked together for a start. The next thing is to eliminate any tendency to lift the skis off the snow as you initiate the turn – lightening the skis, or unweighting, can be done without hopping or bouncing the heels – so that the skis stay in contact with the snow throughout the turn.

The pole plant has now to be timed exactly with the down motion, so that as you come up and extend your whole body forward on the skis, there is an instant reaction to turn the skis. These movements have to be made in a smooth but definite sequence. As you rise up the skis flatten and away downhill they turn, to be immediately followed by you making a downsink, semi-kneeling press forward of the knees towards the tips, transferring more weight pressure to the outer ski in order to maintain the steering or carving of the turn.

This refined form of the parallel swing requires you to think and feel more of making the turns in a fluent and precise manner. Jerky, sudden and jumping movements do not give a good deal of edge control, and block any flowing, flexing and extending of the legs.

In order to link your parallel turns smoothly, you should think of the swing as being the preparation ready to make another turn immediately you have skidded the skis sufficiently across the slope. Then as you steer the tips in the swing, cranking the knees in the direction you wish the skis to go, you gradually bring the outer arm forward to plant the pole at the end of the turn, to trigger off another turn in the opposite direction.

Short parallel swings

Ski-ing down the more difficult ski runs off the top of the mountain will always present you with one or more steep pitches that you have to get down. This is where the ability to make very quick, small radius turns helps you to lose height quickly, and at the same time you are able to brake on your ski edges to check your speed.

Ski down your run to a suitable slope where you can do this *edge check exercise*. Start off in the traverse, not too slowly, then fold the legs quickly to press the heels of the skis downhill into a short skid that will stop as the ski edges bite into the snow. The action is to make a very short sideslip which is stopped by stamping both ski edges into the snow. As your downsink and knee action make the skis check, the arm and pole on the downhill side should be planted hard. You can push off the pole to turn the skis back into the traverse line, standing up ready to make another skid-check-bite coupled with the pole plant. Try it in rhythm across the slope back and forth. Don't sit back on your heels or the sideslip check will be too much and will stop you sliding. This forceful edge-set check is the basis for performing short swings. Choose a moderately steep slope, and by combining the sharp edge-setting action with correctly timed pole plant, you can push off this 'platform' made in the snow, to turn the skis smartly with an up-flex of the legs. The knees again are pressed into the direction of turning the skis quickly back across the slope, so that the ski heels are fanned out and the opposite edges reset into the snow.

As soon as the skis are making their short fanning skid over

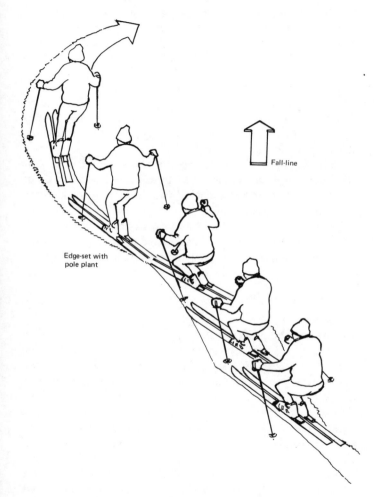

Edge-set with
pole plant

Fall-line

Figure 38. Short swings on a steep slope.

the snow, you should stop the skid with another quick drop by bending knees and ankles, to couple an immediate edge-set check with a pole plant into another short swing. To avoid over-turning the skis, and keep the flow of movements going, keep your hands and poles forward, with your upper body staying in a facing-out down the slope position. At each edge-check plat-form and pole plant you will brake and control your sliding speed. Facing out down the slope enables you to go with your skis and anticipate the turning movements, ready to thrust the skis from one bite in the snow to the next.

As the slope becomes less steep, the edging bite made to slow your skis down will become less pronounced, smoothing out the action into that of the normal parallel turn, or making the rapid leg play of *Wedeln* swings.

If your lower ski tends to break away into a small stem, don't let this worry you – it is the co-ordinating of turning movements that is the essential part of short swinging.

Smoothing out the ski run terrain

Ski-ing down any run, you will not have failed to notice that the more accomplished skiers appear to sit back when they turn the skis. There are several different methods of initiating the turning action into the parallel type turn, and so far you have learned to make your turns by using an up-motion to unweight the skis in order to turn both skis at the same time. You have also used the mogul bumps as an aid to steer your skis round. However, if you use too much unweighting when making the basic parallel swing, the skis will be bounced off the bump, and the best way of controlling them is to keep their soles and edges in contact with the snow all the time, This is when the advanced skier modifies his technique to make a deliberate use of the bumps.

7. Short swing turns

Figure 39. Ski-ing line through bumps.

Figure 40. Pivoting skis on crest of bump.

94

Pivoting or swivelling the skis on moguls

Instead of using a pronounced unweighting motion to turn the skis on the crest of the bump, you must try simply twisting the feet and skis round. Pick out a bump, stand still on the crest and plant your pole on the downhill side. Now with a downsink of the legs only, twist your knees outwards away from the slope and see how easily the tips and heels swivel round. It helps if you plant the pole more downhill from your boots rather than too near the tips, since this gives your upper body a slight anticipated face-out ready to take the turn as it starts, as well as providing a good support as you pivot the skis. If you look down closely at your boots and skis as you twist your knees out from the slope, you will see that the skis roll off their uphill edges, flatten, then start to roll over on to the other edges. This is exactly what you want to happen when you turn. Practice this swivel of the skis by traversing a line of bumps, folding your legs as you ride up on to the bump. Plant the pole and twist the lower leg and boot. Feel the skis turn while you are in the down position. The next part of the turn again is different from the standard parallel turn. To hold the skis onto the snow as they slide off on the down side of the mogul, usually into a hollow-shaped scoop in the snow, you have to stretch your legs out to the side, pushing the skis down and round in the turn. You can do this as an exercise across the bumps, bending and stretching out the legs down the hollows as you pass over them.

The 'Wellen' technique of compensation turns

Using the folding of the legs with correctly placed pole plant as you ride up on to the bump, turn the skis downhill while still

95

in the low squat position. Maintain a hold on the pole plant while you press the knees towards the downhill side. Then, when the skis are pointing directly downhill, stretch out the legs to the outside to keep the skis in contact with the snow and ride into the hollow or mogul trough. When the skis have swung

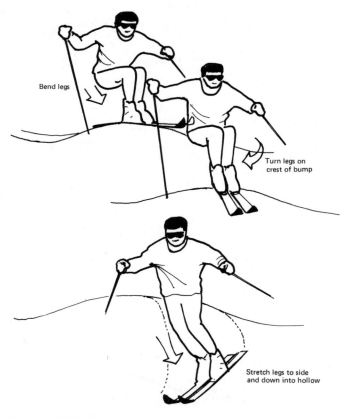

Figure 41. 'Wellen' technique of turning on moguls.

97

8. *Turn over moguls*

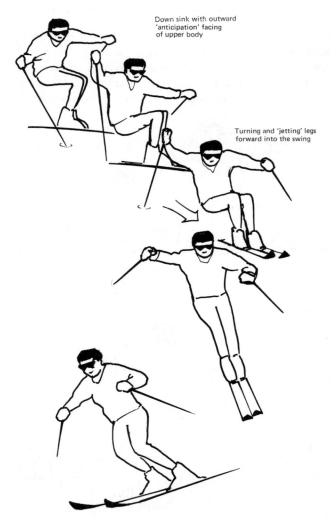

Down sink with outward
'anticipation' facing
of upper body

Turning and 'jetting' legs
forward into the swing

Figure 42. Jet turn sequence movements.

98

round across the bump, then sink down slightly to steer the skis in the normal way, ready to fold and bend the legs on the crest of the next bump that you pick to turn on. As you slide over the mogul hump and fold the legs to absorb the impact of the skis hitting the top, you should stand with your weight evenly on both skis until they are both turned and into the swing part of the turn. The Austrian 'Wellen' technique, as described, is based on the way bumps are run straight. There are many variants to this, the basic method of compensating with the skis and legs for the shape of the snow surface. The French 'Avalement' turn uses a little more anticipation twist at the start of the turn, swallowing up the mogul as before. Jet turns use a similar action, but 'jet' the feet out and forward into the turn after planting the pole. Extreme versions use a sitting back on the heels to pivot the skis round on their backs, shooting out the skis to wheel round off the snow.

Jump turns

The mogul can also be used to practice hopping off the whole ski to turn and land in the opposite direction. Ski up on to the bump and place both poles on the crest well in front of your boots, sink down as the poles are planted followed by a good push off and spring of the legs, to lift-off both skis. Turn the skis immediately downhill to land with them across the slope, sinking down on them to absorb the landing. Although the jump or 'Aerial' turn is not the sort of thing you will want to be doing all the time, it is good practice at movement co-ordination and edge control, as well as being useful if you ski into crusty snow where you have to lift the skis out of the snow to turn them.

Why learn short swings and mogul compensation turns?

Short swings enable you to ski down steeper slopes, losing height directly down the fall-line without picking up speed. Making a long turn on a steep slope will pick up too much speed. You can also negotiate narrow runs, and more difficult slopes and pistes,

Downsink onto both
poles planted

Spring off and turn
skis in the air

Land with a downsink of legs

Figure 43. Jump or 'Aerial' turn off a bump.

that require you to do continuous short check turns from side to side

Turning through the bumps by folding your legs – bending, turning and stretching the legs to follow the undulations of the terrain – helps to keep your skis in constant contact with the snow, giving you edge control to carve and brake without being thrown or bounced off course.

Why become an advanced skier?

You will enjoy the total fun to be had from all that ski-ing offers. The advanced ski-ing stage has been reached when you can apply the technique you've learned to the best advantage according to each situation as it arises. Each run down the snow has to be read, anticipating and looking at the ground ahead. Using up-motion swings where the snow is smooth, folding your legs to compensate and jet the skis round bumps, short swing checks down steep pitches, and stepping up or skating round trouble spots – it's an exciting new sensation. Enjoying ski-ing does not stop at the ability to perform a monotonous series of similar turns in a regular pattern down the slope, although it does require you to be in good physical shape and have just a little aggressiveness in your approach to ski-ing. However, rest assured that the exhilaration of ski-ing breeds enough enthusiasm for you to keep on improving your technique. Above all, advanced ski-ing gives you the chance to enjoy all the skills you have so far acquired to the best of your ability – safely!

Practical pointers

1. Make the quick edge-set check with a downpress on both skis.

2. Keep your hands and poles in front of the body when making *Wedeln* or short swings.

3. In continuous turning technique, the movements are all flowing and in rhythm without any delays.

4. Fold the legs on the bumps, so that your weight is distributed evenly over the whole foot and equally on both feet.

5. Turn the skis on the bump by pressing the upper knee outwards to start the skis pivoting.

Common errors

PARALLEL TURNS – hopping the heels too high off the snow to start the turn.

SHORT SWINGS – overturning the heels of the skis by pushing the skidded swing too far across the slope and sitting back.

Not fanning the heels of the skis enough to make a check so that the skis run out of control.

EDGE-SET CHECKS – not planting the pole exactly at the moment of edge-set bite.

TURNING OVER BUMPS – straightening the legs or standing up before the skis have had time to turn downhill.

Not using the pole plant correctly for support.

5 · The Craft of Ski-ing

There is much more to ski-ing than just learning and perfecting your ski technique. Apart from what you will learn in the ski class, there is a far wider experience to be gained about ski-ing in such matters as snow conditions, piste manners, respect of mountains and weather, and just common sense safety. It is this craft of being aware of, and being able to deal with, these other aspects of ski-ing that is frequently ignored. Ski-ing craft covers many of the unsaid things that skiers do in practice, as well as outlining the courtesy code and safety hints.

Ski-ing in various snow conditions

If you get the urge to explore slopes other than those trails served by the lifts, the snow will certainly be different from the prepared piste. Your knowledge of the fundamentals of ski technique will stand you in good stead, but you must be prepared to adapt and modify the turning technique according to the specific snow conditions. Go with an experienced skier when the conditions are right to ski in untracked snow – but never ski away from the piste alone.

Turning in powder snow

To those skiers who can control their skis in deep snow, ski-ing down in a series of turns in deep powder gives an added dimension to the delights of ski fun. Leaving the marks of the turns you have just carved out of an untracked snow is another experience that gives you a personal inner satisfaction. They are the skier's graffiti written on the slopes to say 'Look, I was here!' It's a special feeling that cannot be obtained from ski-ing on

Stand with equally weighted skis

Use steady body and pole-plant movements

Plane the skis near the surface when turning

Carry the turn swing through with a gradual downsink on both skis

Figure 44. Ski-ing in powder snow.

the piste, where *your* ski marks are erased almost immediately by the passing ski traffic.

There are two types of ski-ing powder snow: turning on the few centimetres of new snow that falls on hard base, and then swinging through fluffy powder that can come up to the waist.

The first is to turn in about 20 cm of new snow if it has fallen on a packed under-surface, such as a ski run. The only modification to using the standard parallel turn is to make your turning movements smoother and more precise over a slightly longer duration of the timing sequence. Stand with your weight pressure over the whole foot, and ski as relaxed as you can, avoiding any hard, jerky and stiff movements. A little anticipation in the turning of the upper body on to the pole plant helps to make a smooth release of the skis into the turn. The ultimate delight of the ski fanatic is to ski fluently in deep powder. You can use all the modern forms of the parallel turn, provided that you maintain your weight pressure on both skis and adjust your stance over the skis so as to allow them to 'plane' through the powder snow. All movements again should be precise, but again not made as quickly or as hard as when you have to use your ski edges on the piste. Squat down over the skis more, ensuring that all the while the ski tips are allowed to float up towards the surface of the snow; press too far forward on the skis and the tips will 'submarine' and dive too deep into the snow. The secret of maintaining good control when turning in deep snow is to avoid any sideways extremes of body position in relation to the planing platform of the skis, and also to try not to over-weight one ski more than the other. The deep sitting-back turns used for ski-ing bumps are ideal for taming the challenge of deep powder. Try it for the first time by choosing a medium angle slope, and ski-ing straight down the fall-line to feel the skis float as you attempt small turning movements. Remember that because the skis have got to slice and plane through the snow, you have got to wait a little longer for your turning movements to take effect. Both skis have to be banked round as the whole ski soles take the weight pressure down on the snow, rather than riding on the edges.

If you fall down in powder snow it can be quite an effort to scramble around and get back upright. You have to shuffle round without tiring yourself out until you can free both skis before attempting to get upright again. Putting a ski back on again can be a nuisance in powder snow, as the ski tends to sink down into the stuff and it is difficult to keep the boot platform free of snow. Cross one ski over the other, to give yourself a base on which to stand while you refix the boot into the bindings.

What skis to use in powder snow

Your short skis will work just as well in powder. A fairly flexible ski is best in the standard length, preferably of a thin section like that of a metal ski, so that there is little side resistance on the skis as they turn. The flex allows the skis to ride higher in the snow, and prevents the tips from diving too deep.

Corn snow ski-ing

Corn or spring snow is formed by the successive melting and freezing of the snow into small ice particles. It is found usually at the end of the ski season when the snow has had time to settle and age into ice granules, and gives excellent ski-ing over its fast surface.

When the sun has warmed up and had the chance to soften up corn snow, it rapidly turns into wet 'mush' snow. To ski through this heavy wet mush, requires more application of strength through the legs to push the skis round into the turns. If necessary stand more or less with evenly weighted skis, especially at the beginning of the turn, using a twist anticipation of the upper body to help release more power to the turning action of the legs. An application of the correct wax will help to cut down the suction effect of the wet snow on the running surface of the skis.

Ski-ing through crusted snow

Crusted snow forms when the surface of a snow layer has been subjected to a thaw, most often by direct exposure of the slope to the sunlight, followed by hard frost. When this hard crust is covering an under-layer of soft or powder snow, the skis tend to break through the surface, making it extremely difficult to ski through. If you are confronted by having to ski down a slope that has turned into 'breakable crust', the only safe way is to get down in a series of traverses, making a stop and stepping or jumping the skis round at the end of each traverse.

Dealing with ice

Ice to the skier means either a very hard frozen snow surface, or actual melted snow patches that have become solid ice. On the hard frozen slope the skis will skid and slide sideways from underneath you if you do not apply correct edge bite control. Apart from the fact that it helps considerably to have your ski edges sharp, you should lean out from the waist more than the normal running position in order to press the whole of your weight down on to the ski. If the skis continue to drift sideways, then try successive quick downsinks on to the skis to give a series of edge checks – making the skis bite for a fraction at each setting. The hardest thing to do is to remain as relaxed as possible and avoid going completely rigid, so as to prevent the skis from skating out completely from under your legs. Turn down the frozen slope by using short swings, so that you are always braking from one edge-set across the slope, quickly fanning the skis round on to the next check. Canting the boots and skis too far over on to their tracking edges will also result in loss of bite into the surface. Ski in a ready flexed position with your weight pressed forward on the forepart of the skis, to avoid the heels sliding away, and keep as much of the ski in contact with the surface as possible.

If you hit a patch of pure water ice, the only safe way is to be prepared to let the skis drift across the area of ice until you can skid down on to a more granular surface on which to brake. Ski-ing on ice is not very pleasant, and the answer is to try to avoid the hard polished areas, picking out instead the slope surfaces that may be rougher in texture and will therefore give you the best grip.

Piste ski-ing hints

There are problems and hazards that arise when ski-ing down ski runs or trails that are not catered for in the normal process of learning to ski. The shape of the terrain, or the restriction on a ski run by rocks or woods, can present a fear that somehow stylish ski technique is not going to succeed in getting you down this particular passage. These are the practical answers to some of the more common hazards.

Narrow runs through woods

Runs through woods come in different forms – some are steep and smooth, while others traverse more across the slope and are rutted. The uphill side of these runs have a steep hostile bank of tree roots and rocks that stick out ready to snag the unwary

Figure 45. Ski-ing down a narrow wood run.

ski tip, while to ski down the middle may be too fast with your skis parallel and trapped in the ruts, and too smooth to snow-plough down in control. The answer here is to steer your-self towards the lower, downhill edge of the run. Usually this lower edge is lined by a bank of loose or churned up snow that has been scuffed out of the middle of the run by other skiers fighting to stay in control. Place your outside ski in a half-stem over this edge of the run so that you can brake with this ski on the loose snow. It needs only the part of the ski under your foot to be in contact with the snow, so do not become worried if the tip and heel of the ski is off the snow. You will be surprised how slowly and easily you can negotiate these awesome pass-ages in this way, as long as you have enough confidence to stay out on the edge, especially if it drops away steep into the woods.

Ski pole riding

If the path is a hollowed out shape of hard snow (that makes it almost impossible to snowplough the heels of the skis up the curved sides) then resort to using your poles to slow down. Place both poles in one hand and press the points down into the snow, with the other hand held roughly half way, so that the poles are across your body, just like paddling a canoe. In this way you can lean on the poles to brake. The other way to use your poles, which is frowned on by the experts, is to place both poles between your legs, grip the handles firmly, and sit down on them to make the points again bite into the snow between the heels of your stemmed out skis. Sit down harder and you slow down. It's not particularly kind to your poles, but it works.

Steep funnel or 'Gunbarrel' runs

Where the ski run is channelled into a narrow gulley or ravine by the very nature of the mountainside, making it the only place to descend, then the run is usually steep, and shaped in big moguls. Unless you can stay in the bed of the gully, making continuous short turns and soaking up the bumps correctly at each swing, then the simple course is to ski just on to one side of the funnel and side-slip down. A quick look down the run will give you an idea of which is the best side to skid down on. Keep your upper ski advanced; holding the skis apart may give you a more relaxed stance. Once you are losing height, it is the same as doing a side-slip diagonally across a normal level slope, and you can guide yourself by giving a dig or push with the poles on the uphill side. A quick prod with the ski pole can help you steer the skid round bumps or rocks, without the need to turn. If you get cramp in your feet or want a rest,

Figure 46. Ski-ing slowly down a 'gunbarrel' run.

pick a spot of loose snow on the top of a bump to stop on. Always keep one eye on the slope above for other skiers coming down.

Ski-ing over bumpy or switchback terrain

Taking a straight line over a series of undulations, it is quite easy to be thrown as the skis hit the bumps and to lose the sequence of bending and stretching the legs. To avoid being pitched forward or knocked backwards, advance one ski about a boot length forward, so that you ride from one foot to the other and stay in balance. When ski-ing into a deep hollow do the same action, but lean back to be ready for the skis slowing down.

Ski-ing off the piste into deep snow

Turning off the packed snow into the untracked snow at the side, requires you to be on your guard ready for the skis slowing down. Compensate your ski-ing position to remain in balance by bending your knees and ankles to squat slightly and sit back, so that as the skis decelerate on diving into the snow you will not be pitched forward on your face. Keep your hands and poles low, avoiding lifting them too high. You must lean back in the same way when ski-ing onto patches of wet snow or grass and heather, where the skis will suddenly slow or even stop sliding.

Hitting hard snow or ice

The reverse is necessary when the skis suddenly go faster. Try to lean well forward and go with the skis. If you see a patch of ice or you are ski-ing back onto the packed piste surface after turning through loose deep snow, then sink down by pressing the knees forward, lowering your centre of gravity. This will give you a more stable body position ready to take the sudden increase in speed.

Deep ruts or 'tramlines'

Deep rutted tracks occur where the run narrows, or on the tow track. If your skis drop into the tracks and you are not very happy at being locked into the ruts, then step one ski at a time out of the track in quick succession. Make for any loose snow that is on the side of the run, to ride at least one ski as a means of checking your speed.

Hop and spring before reaching the crest

Extend the legs after the crest has been cleared

Figure 47. Pre-jumping a bump at speed.

Pre-jumping humps

Taking a slope in a straight run at speed, or schussing, requires you to lower your centre of gravity by slightly crouching in a forward position. Keep your hands and poles low, ready to help in keeping your balance. Hitting a large bump at speed is liable to make you unintentionally airborne, as you fly off the downhill side. To remain in turning control of your skis they have to stay in contact with the snow, and on approaching the lip of a hump or sudden drop off give a small hop with both skis before they hit the top or crest of the hump. This pre-jump will allow the skis to settle back down on the snow immediately after the crest, ready to take any avoiding action that may be necessary. Never ski blindly, or jump off a bump, when you cannot see if the snow is clear of rocks or another skier lying down on the snow.

Figure 48. Picking a good line down a piste or ski trail.

Picking a good line

Just because the ski resort has groomed out and designed ski runs and trails down the mountain does not mean that all you have to do is to ski blindly down anywhere on the run. The skier who is constantly searching and looking ahead to choose the best line down the run, is exercising yet another facet of the craft of ski-ing. Anticipation of the best line on the terrain is coupled with being able to train your eye to seek out the easiest snow to turn on, and also to recognise what the condition of the snow is ahead. Reading the snow ahead will instinctively put you in a pre-warned position that will at least have you ready to deal with any quick decision that may be necessary. The skier who develops a quick recognition and appreciation of what lies ahead in his path is obviously a safer skier than one who skis into difficult snow or terrain, unaware of the hazards that can lie in wait.

In any case, picking out the best line is part of the enjoyment of ski-ing, as you look out for any variation that can give you a pleasant run, instead of plunging down without thinking and getting into difficulties.

Bad weather ski-ing

It has to snow sometime in a ski resort, and it is unfortunate if you happen to have your holiday when the weather has decided to change for the worse. However, you can still ski when it is snowing, and with a bit more caution and adequate clothing, it can still be fun. It is the 'white out' conditions of snowing and mist that can make ski-ing down unpleasant and unnerving. The problem of this weather is that because everything looks a grey-white, snow surface, bumps and hollows, and all other features of the surroundings merge into one. The inability to see and register the lie of the slope ahead will make you want to stiffen up on the defensive, not knowing what is coming up to meet your skis. Try to remain relaxed and ski slowly so that you are ready to take any unexpected shock as the skis ride over bumps and hollows that are difficult to see. Ski with a companion, changing over the lead in turn, so that you can get an idea of the line of the slope from the other person's skis. Wear yellow-tinted goggles to help your vision.

Remember to warm up before ski-ing down

On your first run down, particularly in cold weather, do a few squats to flex the legs fully, or any leg bend and stretch exercises – jump up and down to get the circulation going and warm up cold muscles. If you are self-conscious about performing gymnastics in front of a ski lift audience, then side-stepping up from the lift exit will soon have you warmed up – taking a short climb before you ski down. Ski-ing straight off down with tight, cold muscles can be dangerous – your reflexes and leg actions are sluggish, and a mistake in your ski-ing could be painful.

Be a safe skier

Oddly enough, most physical sports need to have an element of risk in them to provide a stimulus of enjoyment. In ski-ing the risks come from falling down and the dangers that arise from being in a mountain environment. Fortunately you do not have to go out and hurt yourself to enjoy ski-ing, as much as the ski-cartoonists would have you believe! But accidents do happen, and to exercise a little safety first will make your holiday a pleasurable one, rather than having a sad ending. Just to dispel any gloom that might arise, careful statistical recordings have proved that the proportion of accidents to the numbers of people ski-ing is extremely small – something like two people in every 1,000 injure themselves, and these injuries are only minor ones, like a strain or bruising. Of the serious injuries, such as a fracture, the proportion is five times smaller in risk, and with the developments in equipment design and ski technique this danger is further eliminated. Most accidents can be prevented with a little common sense and a few simple precautions.

Check your release bindings

The correct adjustment of release bindings is one way of reducing the risk of injury to yourself, should you fall awkwardly. The designers of ski bindings try to ensure that the mechanisms operate for your safety, but cannot make them foolproof, and it is finally left to you to see that the setting of the release is correctly adjusted. Always have a quick look to see that the setting has not changed, whenever you put your skis on. The vibrations of actually ski-ing, plus any knocks the skis may get while in a ski rack or being carried, can change the setting of the binding. A loosely set binding can be just as much a potential danger as a binding that is screwed up solid. With the large number of different kinds of bindings now on the market, it is impossible to give a detailed guide as to how to check ski bindings. You should make a special effort to be shown how your particular ski binding operates and to understand the adjustment points.

Ski bindings can release in various ways – the toe piece can swing open at various angles, while the heel fastening usually acts as the 'docking' device with overriding release features. A rough check can be made by gripping the toe piece with your hand and twisting the device – you should be able to turn the binding even though it may take some effort. Alternatively put the ski on and knock the toe part of your boot with the free foot to see if the binding show signs of releasing. The heel binding can be tried by asking someone to stand on the back of your skis, then by leaning forward see if there are signs that the mechanism is going to allow your boot to come free. It is emphasised that these checks are only a very rough guide, and cannot replace the correct visual check according to the manufacturer's recommendations. Finally ice can freeze up the mechanisms, so keep your bindings free of packed snow and well greased. Clean off all the snow from your boot soles before stepping into the bindings.

Other equipment checks

Apart from the ski bindings, there are other parts of your equipment that need a quick check now and then, to see that they are not going to cause you to take a fall or injure yourself. Ski poles that are bent could be fractured, and cause a nasty injury if they suddenly break. If the snow basket or ring on the end of the pole becomes broken then have it replaced – it may snag up on a projection while you are ski-ing. Have a look at your ski soles regularly, a broken steel edge or a chunk out of the running surface, can drastically affect the sliding of the ski, perhaps just when you want to take avoiding action! Your ski boots can have broken clips or fastenings that will snag up, for instance on your partner's boots while riding a ski-tow.

Accident procedure

If you are involved in an accident, or called up to help an injured person, the following tips will help to protect and render immediate treatment.

Remove the person's skis and plant them in a X form above where the skier is lying, as a warning to other skiers to keep clear.

Keep the person warm, place ski jackets, gloves, etc., under and around the body, without moving the person more than is strictly necessary.

Do not remove the boots.

Don't give any drinks, alcohol is strictly forbidden.

Administer any immediate first aid, clear any restricted breathing, stop bleeding, etc., and send or call for the ski patrol, giving the exact location of the accident.

If you are hurt, then try to remain calm, and do not refuse the help of the ski patrol.

Avalanche danger

Many people are under the impression that avalanches only occur high up among the sharp inaccessible peaks of the mountains. What is not fully realized by a lot of skiers is that a beautiful, innocent looking slope of sparkling snow can suddenly slide off and catch the unwary. While as a learner skier you will only be concerned with ski-ing on the packed snow of the piste, it is prudent to be aware of the hidden dangers that certain snow slopes may hide. Almost any open slope without woods or rock outcrops, over an angle of 20° (a medium angled slope), is liable to avalanche given the right conditions. This is not to say that easy gradient slopes will not slide. If the snow is lying at a shallow angle on a grassy slope that becomes lubricated by melted snow, it may slide when the extra weight of a skier suddenly comes on to it.

If there has been considerable new snowfall, you can assume that the avalanche hazard is high. Likewise a quick drop or rapid rise in temperature affects the structure of lying snow, and this adds to the hazard. Avoid lee slopes sheltered by ridges and shoulders of the mountainside, where the wind can cause huge masses of snow to accumulate.

Avalanches occur when masses of snow become unstable, owing to the weight of the snow and gravity overcoming the forces holding it, with the result that they slide down to a less steeply inclined level. There are three major avalanche categories: dry powder snow which comes down in airborne blasts, wet snow sliding sluggishly, and slabs of compacted snow that break up into big blocks. The latter slab avalanche hazard is difficult to detect, even by experts, and is the cause of many accidents involving avalanches.

If you are ski-ing on un-pisted snow, and suddenly feel a 'crump' under your skis, beware – you may trigger off a slide. Likewise keep a wary lookout on the slopes above you: it's the snow that comes from above that is going to trap you.

The following are general hints to observe should you be likely to come into an avalanche situation.

Take due regard of all ski area notices regarding avalanche danger, or ask advice about conditions if you are going to a specific area.

Never ski alone away from patrolled areas.

Keep high on ridges, avoiding corniced and lee slopes.

If you have to cross a suspect slope, go one at a time from one safe point to the next safe feature. Go on foot rather than ski, preferably straight down than a traverse. Trail an avalanche cord or suitable line, loosen ski bindings, rucksack straps, and pole straps from wrists. Fasten up jacket and hood, cover up mouth and nose.

If you are caught in a slide, get rid of skis and rucksack, try to 'swim' keeping your mouth and nose covered up, don't panic, and as the slide slows down try and create a space round your face and chest.

If you see someone caught in an avalanche, make a quick note of where their last position was, mark this point. Send for immediate help, after first checking quickly for any visible sign of the victim, probing with reversed ski poles. Don't endanger yourself or others to further avalanche.

The skier's courtesy and safety code

To protect the safety of skiers and to give them the maximum enjoyment, an internationally agreed code of conduct has been formulated by the Federation Internationale de Ski (F.I.S.); extracts as follows:

1. The slower skier always has the right of way.
2. Always ski in control. Be able to stop when necessary and avoid other skiers.
3. An overtaking skier shall avoid the skier below or beyond him, in a manner that will not cut across the path of the slower skier.
4. Stop on the side of the piste or trail, never in a position where you will impede or block the passage of other skiers.
5. Do not walk on the piste without skis; if for some reason you have to walk on the trail do so on the edge.
6. Observe all guide signs and information boards; they are for your protection.
7. A skier starting off or joining another piste or trail junction shall look first to be sure the way is clear before moving out into the middle of the run.
8. Use a retaining strap or device, to prevent a ski from running loose down the slope if you take a fall.
9. Give way to the beginner skier, his control may not be as good as yours.
10. If you see or suspect an accident, enquire if you can help,

co-operate with the ski patrol, and if you are not required to help them ski well clear.

Finally, stop ski-ing when you are tired – taking that 'last run' after a hard day can be tempting fate!

Ski piste and trail markers

There are many different signs and markers on pistes and lift systems. They range from indicating the standard of the run, to safety signs and ski traffic directions.

The run-standard markers in Alpine countries are usually round discs with the name or number of the run on the different colour standard background. Yellow is the colour for the easy run, Blue for the easy to intermediate difficult run, Red for the difficult run, and Black for the most difficult runs. In North American ski areas the markings of ski trail standards are different. A green square sign points out the easy runs, a yellow triangle for difficult runs, and a blue circle for the hardest trails, with a red diamond shape indicating extra caution.

Pistes that are closed for some reason or other, perhaps bare of snow or in danger of avalanching, are marked with signs: Gesperrt (German), Fermé (French), Chiuso (Italian), and usually in understandable Closed.

To guide and control ski-ing traffic on the pistes there are several direction signs, and it is worthwhile taking a note of what they mean, before meeting them for the first time on your way down a run!

Think about yourself !

A final word of advice on this business of being a safe skier – be personally prepared!

Physique and fitness While you don't have to be a super-human

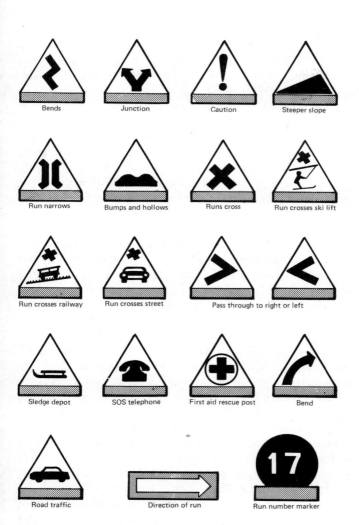

Bends

Junction

Caution

Steeper slope

Run narrows

Bumps and hollows

Runs cross

Run crosses ski lift

Run crosses railway

Run crosses street

Pass through to right or left

Sledge depot

SOS telephone

First aid rescue post

Bend

Road traffic

Direction of run

Run number marker

Figure 49. International Ski Run Marking Signs.

being to be able to ski, it is wise to consider your own personal limitations before trying to emulate the experts or fitter skiers. Everyone can enjoy ski-ing in his own way by not over-doing it – even some blind people and folk with only one leg get pleasure from ski-ing in their own special way. If you are past your youth, take it steady for the first few days. At a high resort, your 'ticker' has to work a little harder to pump around the same oxygen you would need at sea-level. Give yourself time to adjust to the sudden bout of exercise, especially if you are not used to jumping up and down, and suddenly falling about on the floor! Pre-ski conditioning exercises are dealt with later.

Sunburn and glare   Sun reflecting off snow can give you a very uncomfortable burn, the clear air at altitude adding to the sun's power on unprotected skin. Use a suitable cream on all exposed skin areas – not forgetting ears, back of neck and nostrils. Avoid having your lips burned by using lip salve liberally smeared on.

In any bright sunlight use sunglasses or tinted goggles. Snowblindness is a very painful, if temporary, ailment that can be easily avoided.

Feet and ankles   If you are not used to wearing heavy boots – that means just about everybody – then be prepared by either wearing your own boots a few times before you go away on holiday, or taking along some soft spongy material, anklets, crépe bandaging – in fact anything that will pad out a sore ankle. If you are going to ski correctly with a bend in your ankle, pressing forward onto the tongue of the boot can be painful on sensitive skin areas of the foot. By cutting out a hole in soft padding material, like corn plasters, a sore spot can be relieved to make ski-ing comfortable again.

Sore throats   Breathing in, shouting and laughing in the general exuberance of ski-ing in the dry atmosphere of high mountains can cause sore throats. Take plenty of liquid refreshment;

especially have something to drink by your bed at night in case you wake up with a dry throat.

Tummy bugs With the changes in diet and water, it is worthwhile taking along suitable medicaments to combat any attacks of stomach upset.

Insurance protection It is very advisable to take out a special insurance cover to protect yourself, should you have the misfortune to be involved in an accident. The expense of medical treatment, rescue and possible third party claims can be frighteningly high, and although the fault may not be yours – some other idiot out of control crashing into you – the small outlay on the premium for suitable insurance is well worth while. Your travel agent or the Ski Club of Great Britain can give you further particulars of ski-ing insurance.

6 · Getting Prepared

Ski equipment and clothing

As with any other sport, having the right equipment and clothing can affect the degree of your performance. Apart from the quality and type of equipment you choose, there is also the question of looking after it once you have started to use it. Ski equipment takes quite an amount of wear and tear which will affect its performance, no matter how good a skier you are. However, with the use of modern materials the maintenance and serviceability of ski gear does not present the problems it used to do a few years ago. In fact there is such a variety of equipment now available, most of it first class, that choice can present quite a baffling problem. Although skis now come in all shapes and sizes from short, fat skis to long and thin ones, there has been no major change in the basic design that emerged from the experiments of Sondre Nordheim, in Norway during the mid-1800's. Clothing too has been subjected to change without losing its functional requirements. Gone are the days of heavy tweed knickerbockers and baggy pants, to be replaced by a bewildering array of very fashionable yet practical garments.

Choosing skis

The basic commodity of ski-ing comes in several sizes, and for several different purposes. There are skis made specially for different racing requirements – Slalom skis are stiff and narrow

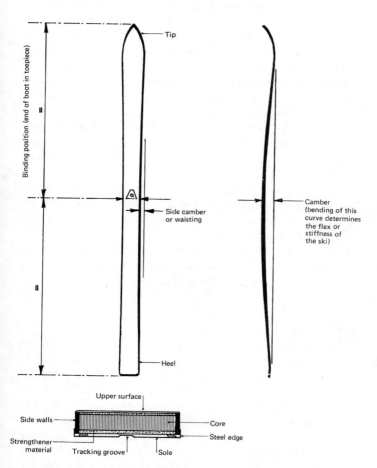

Side camber or waisting

Camber (bending of this curve determines the flex or stiffness of the ski)

Tip

Heel

Binding position (end of boot in toepiece)

Upper surface

Side walls

Core

Strengthener material

Steel edge

Tracking groove

Sole

Section through the middle of a ski

Figure 50. Skis – parts.

in the middle, Giant Slalom skis are not so stiff, and skis for downhill racing are longer and wider with even more flex. In addition there are skis for cross-country ski-ing that are very thin and light, and now the new ranges of shorter skis specially made for learning in graduated lengths. But by far the most popular type of skis are those made especially for the recreational skier. They combine a good many of the features to be found in racing skis, that are of an advantage to the needs of the skier only interested in pleasure ski-ing. Briefly a ski should have these optimum features – be able to turn easily, hold well on hard snow or ice, perform well in deep snow, and have good vibration damping and stability at speed.

If you are a beginner to the sport, choosing a pair of skis needs careful consideration. Do you hire the equipment for your first try, or are you keen enough to want to buy a pair of skis? Either way, with hiring being favourite for a first-timer, ensure that you use a short ski, that is one that does not come any longer than your own height. Gone are the days of reaching up to the sky to curl your fingers over the tip, to see if that was your ski length! In fact ski manufacturers are now producing fewer skis in their longer sizes (over 200 cm.), such is the sensible attitude towards the use of the shorter ski.

Buying skis depends to a large extent on how much you are willing to pay for them. Skis are manufactured in wood, plastic, metal and glass-fibre. With all the slick coloured plastic finishes that the manufacturer uses on the skis, it is difficult at a first glance to see which are the cheaper or more expensive skis, when they are lined up in the sports shop ski rack. It is quite easy to be influenced by the coloured design on the ski's top surface. The cheaper skis are still made from wood, although with the development of man-made materials, more skis are being made from the combination of several materials. The more expensive skis are made from laminations of strong materials such as metal and resin impregnated glass fibre, by a highly controlled process. Although all skis now have a plastic running sole, reducing the need for continual waxing to make the ski slide, the cheaper ski will only give you a limited period of service before it loses its flex. The more expensive ski will give you better turning qualities – smoothness in flexing and bite – coupled with longer service. Don't be palmed off with someone else's cast-off skis, they may be far too long, twisted out of shape, and have had a hidden repair job done on them for good measure!

When you select a pair of skis you should look to see first if they are really a pair! Check that the number stamped or printed on them is the same, which means that at least in the factory they were 'mated'. Now look down the sole of both skis from the tip to see if the ski is straight. Put both skis together, soles facing one another, and squeeze them at their mid-point. Then there should be a spring resistance, but when fully closed the soles and edges should be flat together along the whole length. Hold the skis sideways so that you can try to see light through the crack between the closed skis. Any big gap at the tip or heel may mean one ski has more flex camber than the other. Flexing the ski by holding the tip in one hand and pressing the centre down with the other hand, requires a life-time of experience at testing the flex values! All it really shows you is that the ski will bend! Check the steel edges on the ski sole. The cheaper skis usually have screwed on edge-segments, whilst the more expensive skis have the steel edge bonded into the sole – see that they are flush with the running surface. Top surfaces are mostly a scratch resistant plastic covering; on some cheaper skis this upper surface can be only a painted finish. When you finally buy a pair of skis, do make a note of their number, it makes it much easier to trace them should you lose them or have them stolen.

Figure 51. Release bindings, directions of release.

Bindings

The binding fastening the boot to the ski has undergone highly technological development since the first leather straps and thongs. In the interests of safety, much has been done to enable the boot to release from the ski in the event of a severe twist or impact force. The simple requirements that you should look for in a ski binding are that they should hold your boot firmly on the ski, be easy to get into and out of, have an uncomplicated adjustment, and are not too heavy.

Release bindings are made basically in two types – the step-in binding, with which you clamp your boot onto the ski by a mechanism at the toe and heel and step out again by pressing or lifting a release trigger, and the now not so familiar cable binding, where a cable and lever tighten the heel of the boot down onto the toe piece.

The ski shop can advise you as to the merits of the various makes of bindings, cost again determining the quality and service you can expect to get from them. The fitting of the

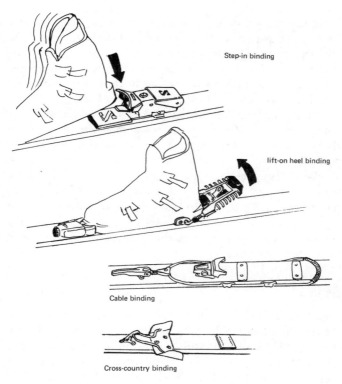

Step-in binding

lift-on heel binding

Cable binding

Cross-country binding

Figure 52. Types of ski bindings.

bindings is best left to the ski shop, but as a rough guide the
toe piece is centred on the half-way point of the ski, measured
from the heel to tip. Place the toe of the boot on this point and
butt up the toe piece to the boot, then screw down. Fix the heel
fastening afterwards, allowing for adjustment either to tighten
or to slacken the setting. Don't always take the markings that
the ski maker may put on the ski for the binding position as

being correct. Check by measuring for yourself. If you have larger than normal boots (size 11 upwards), then put the binding one centimetre forward towards the ski tip. Likewise if your feet are small (size 6 and below) put the binding back one cm. Use a suitable strap or clip to retain the ski to your foot, if it comes off.

Release bindings are sometimes wrongly referred to as 'safety bindings', leading to the assumption that they should always fail safe in the event of the user falling down. It is virtually impossible to design the binding that will meet all shocks and loadings of normal ski-ing, and also differentiate between these and the pressure loadings of all possible injuries. Some painful falls occur at very slow speeds, that may not trigger off the release. The answer is to keep your bindings carefully adjusted, and in good order, so that they are at their maximum efficiency in your time of need!

Boots

Your foot and the ski contact – the better you can 'feel' the ski through your foot and boot, the better your ski control will be. A snug-fitting boot will transmit this feeling much more than a loose-fitting one, and so can be regarded as a very important part of ski equipment. Over the past few years the shape of ski boots has undergone a drastic change, the back of the boot reaching high up to the calf to aid the skier in performing advanced ski technique. As clips have replaced the chore of lacing to fasten up the boots, so have plastic moulded materials gradually taken over from leather in the manufacture of boots. Don't be put off by all the hardwear of the modern ski boot; it may look like something out of space, but it is functional, being designed for ski-ing and not walking! Ski boots are made stiff and rigid so that when you turn your foot over to edge the ski,

Advanced skiing boot with high-back

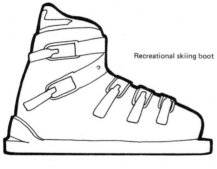

Recreational skiing boot

Cross-country boot

Figure 53. Types of ski boots.

133

there is an immediate response without the boot folding up. But the insides are well padded, with various forms of custom fitting of the inners available in injected foam or otherwise self-forming to the shape of the foot. Wear the socks you will use to go ski-ing when you go to try on a new pair of boots. The boots should give a firm, snug fit, the toes should be just clear of the end of the boot – but you should not be able to move your heel up inside the boot when it is clipped up tight.

Ski poles

Nearly all ski poles are made of tapered metal tubing, and it is just a matter of individual choice which design takes your fancy. The snow ring or basket at the end of the pole offers an array of design shapes, and is mostly made for planting on to packed piste snow. If you go touring into deep snow then a slightly larger snow ring will be an advantage. The grip must fit snugly into the hand, and an adjustable strap is useful.

Choose the length of pole by placing the point near your feet and putting the handle under your armpit. The grip should be clear of being tight under your arm by about 5 cm. (2 in.).

Care and maintenance of skis

The life of your skis, together with their running performance, will be greatly increased if you take good care of them. These small jobs are not very difficult to do, and do not require a range of special tools. Pack them in a ski bag or cover them up in some way when travelling any distance. This will keep dirt off them, and also protect them from the general knocking about skis can get when in transit. Salt spray from winter roads is particularly cruel to steel edges and other exposed metal parts, if they are not covered up.

Check *bindings* for loose screws and fittings, because the flexing and vibrations of actual ski-ing can unscrew fastenings. Grease the working parts with anti-freeze grease. Have a look to see that the retaining straps are not being worn away, so that they will not snap just when you want them to do their job.

Skis – keep the steel edges well honed by filing down with a single cut medium grade file preferably. Sharpen on the side of the ski exactly square to the sole. Run the file along the bottom, sole side, of the edge to take out any nicks or burrs. Repair any scratches or deep grooves in the sole by melting a repair stick of the appropriate plastic material into the damage. A soldering iron is the best medium, but you can light the stick and let it drip on to the sole to fill in the groove. When this has set, scrape off with a knife or sharp straight edge, and finally polish smooth with wire wool or some other abrasive material that is not too coarse. Polish the upper surfaces of the skis with a normal brand of wax polish.

The screwed-on type of steel edge requires constant attention to see that the screws are not standing proud of the surface. This type of edge is easily replaced, carefully plugging up the screw holes first of all. The edge that is bonded in is very difficult to repair if it has taken a bad knock. Use an epoxi resin glue to repair any edges that have split or opened up from the body of the ski, and this goes for de-lamination small splits or if the plastic sole is lifting up. Clean out the part to be bonded, removing all bits of dirt, etc., fill with the resin, and clamp up firmly after covering the area in newspaper so that removal of the clamps or blocks is not made more difficult by surplus glue oozing out and gluing everything up solid! On cheaper skis the metal tip protectors can get worn and knocked, so that nasty sharp corners and burrs of the metal are a potential danger.

Waxing skis – although modern skis have very high frictional

135

resistant plastic soles, it is still advisable to wax the running surface to get the best possible sliding performance according to the snow conditions. In addition it is a protection for the ski sole.

Ski waxes are made in several different kinds, colour-coded according to the temperature and state of the snow. Having chosen your wax, it is best applied hot by melting it in an old container. Paint the wax on when it is hot (not boiling!) with a soft brush that is just wide enough to cover the ski bottom. Paint on in single strokes of about 15 cm. long, starting from the heel and overlapping each previous stroke, right up to the tip. You can also iron on wax by using an old flat iron or a special waxing iron, melting the wax on the side of the iron to drip on to the ski, then smoothing out with the hot iron. Scrape down the sole afterwards with a clean, straight steel edge – a knife held upright, the side of a chisel, or even the steel edge of the other ski – so that the wax is smoothed down, removing any lumps and surplus wax that may have blobbed on to the sole. Finally, clean off the wax that has covered up the steel edges. Before waxing always repair the sole and sharpen up the edges first. Remove all traces of old wax by scraping it off.

Storing skis at the end of the season is not the problem it used to be. Wood skis still need to be clamped together with a block placed in their centre, in order to hold the shape. The modern moulded skis are shaped for life, so clamping up and blocking is not really necessary. Rub a paraffin wax on the steel edges to protect from rust. New skis should always have an application of hot wax on the soles before they are used.

Silver wax – the 'standby' wax of most recreation skiers – can only be rubbed on cold directly to the ski sole.

Ski boots – only leather boots require an application of ordinary boot polish to keep them waterproof. The all-plastic and plastic/leather laminated boots need nothing more than a wipe down, but care must be taken with how much walking you do in them – not that it is possible to walk very far in today's 'wonder boots'! If you wear down the toe and heel of the sole, apart from the boot not fitting correctly into the binding, repair is just about impossible.

Ski clothing

Before you get carried away with the array of ski clothing that is now displayed, remember that ski-ing can be very cold and wet! Think of function before fashion, and if you can combine the two then so much the better.

Ski pants come in all designs. The standard type is tapered into the boot with trousers flared over the top of the boot, zipped up and fastened over the boot clips, knickerbockers and nylon padded all in one suit. Whatever you choose should be windproof and waterproof.

Ski jackets or anoraks should be warm, and again wind and water resistant. Avoid pseudo-ski jackets, which may be alright for casual wear but have a nasty habit of falling apart as soon as you give them some tough ski-ing treatment. The colours and styles of ski-wear are now endless, and most of them have been designed to retain functional qualities with fashion tastes – plenty of zipped pockets and not too bulky. The use of wet-look nylon has been discouraged on account of its dangers if you fall down – the shiny finish acts like a good ski wax, and you just keep on sliding. Now manufacturers have produced anti-skid materials that are well worth considering when you choose a new outfit. Underneath all the overgarments, wool is still the best thing to wear for warmth. Long pants to cover the legs, with one pair of ski socks sufficient for the feet. If you suffer from cold feet wear a thinner pair of socks as an extra – socks are for the insides of ski pants and not untidily rolled

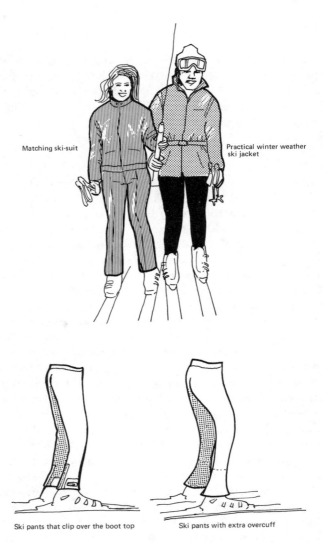

Matching ski-suit

Practical winter weather ski jacket

Ski pants that clip over the boot top

Ski pants with extra overcuff

Figure 54. Clothing.

138

up over the top of the boots. There are lots of multi-coloured roll-neck shirts to wear, with thin wool sweaters worn over the top – two thin sweaters being often better than one huge thick jersey. You can then always take one off if you get too warm.

A warm woollen hat or headband to keep your ears from getting frozen, or to hold your hair in place, is also necessary. As for your hands, gloves look smarter and you can grip your pole handle comfortably, but for some people a mitt without fingers may be warmer, and if it is very cold you can wear a thin pair of wool gloves inside a ski mitt.

A lunch bag, often referred to as a 'bum bag', fastened around the waist, will hold all the little extras that you may need while ski-ing. Wax, cream, spare goggles or glasses, extra strap, plasters, etc., plus your lunch should fit into the bag.

Getting fit

As said before, the skiers who are in a reasonable physical condition, are going to be able to ski and enjoy ski-ing more than those who have not prepared themselves for unaccustomed exercise. There has always been a lot of advice given about pre-ski exercising, but it is true to say that only a minority of skiers are keen enough to dedicate time to a specific conditioning plan. To most of us – the lazy majority – a plan of exercising each day for weeks before the holiday, holds visions of having to strip down and apply yourself to a training schedule like an Olympic athlete! So the answer is to cheat your way into doing extra exercise, or devise some other way that does not need the same dedicated application.

Casually getting into shape Really any activity that will bring on a warm glow to your body, and make you breathe a bit harder than usual, is better than doing nothing. Walk with a brisk step, picking hills both up and down, and stairs, and if you can break out into the odd jog now and then all the better. Cut out a fare stage on the bus into and from work for instance. Riding a bicycle, with the saddle lower than normal, is excellent training for ski-ing, and saves bus fares as well! This goes for most other recreational sports, like golf, ice-skating, squash, tennis and swimming.

There are some exercises that you can do while carrying out the normal daily routine, such as standing in a queue, walking up steps, moving about in the kitchen, or just looking at the television. When standing still anywhere, lift one leg off the ground for a while, then repeat with the other leg, then go a bit further and, bending down slightly again, stand on either leg for a while. Walk up stairs and steps with your toes right on the edge of the step. When sitting on a chair, lean back and lift both legs off the floor, rest, then repeat. If you have new ski boots, try to find time to wear them for half an hour or so each day during the immediate weeks before you go ski-ing. Clomping around the house is an exercise in itself, apart from getting tender ankles used to the boots.

If you feel like just going a stage further then the following exercises will be directly beneficial.

Skipping Rope skipping requires very little space, and is one of the best all-round conditioning workouts that you can do. Skip as an alternate jogging step, varying the rhythm by fast and slow bursts. It's good for the arms, breathing and of course the legs, as well as working up a healthy sweat! 10 to 15 mins.

Squats Stand with feet slightly apart, squat down with hands on hips. Ten times. Then walk or waddle around in all directions still in the squat position. Finally hop forward, to the side and backwards in the squat.

Press-ups Down in the squat, place both hands on the floor and hop both legs out straight behind you, hop back again into the squat position. Five times. Hop out stretched out again,

Skipping

Squats and hops

Press-ups

Trunk and arm circling

Sit-ups

Figure 55. Pre-ski exercises.

and bend the arms to lower the body, press up five times. (You can cheat a bit by pressing up with your knees on the floor!)

Trunk twisting   Stand feet apart, bend down with hands just brushing the floor, and with the help of your arms circle your body to one side, reaching up and over to twist down on the opposite side. Five times in each direction.

Sit-ups   Sit on the floor, hook your toes under a chair or anything that will support your feet as you lie straight back. With hands clasped behind your neck sit upright and return slowly to lie down again. Five times.

Artificial ski slopes

Using an artificial ski slope, if you have one nearby, will give you valuable feel of ski-ing apart from the exercise. While it is not exactly the same as ski-ing on snow, a course of about six hourly lessons will save you valuable learning time when on the snow. Some skiers have found that as much as three days in learning technique can be gained by having had a course on an artificial slope. Certainly you should be able to start at least

Figure 56. Artificial slope matting.

one class up from the beginners. The ski instruction of the basic technique manoeuvres are just the same as you would learn on snow, although the skis do not slide quite as fast as when you are on snow.

The materials used for artificial slopes are mainly bristles of nylon or moulded plastics, and are a little bit harder to fall on than snow, so you should wear old clothes with good mitts to protect your hands in case you take a tumble. The small slopes are only good enough for learning the rudimentaries of ski-ing control, whereas you really need a slope of at least 100 metres to give any good running practice. Information about artificial ski slopes can be obtained from the National Ski Federation.

Grass ski-ing

Simulated ski-ing can be had by using small roller skis or caterpillar type roller tracks fitted to the boots. In this way, you

Figure 57. Grass skis.

can 'ski' or trundle down smooth grassy slopes to give similar practice and exercise that is useful for getting into shape for ski-ing. There is now quite a following for grass ski-ing as a recreation, and several meetings, where racing and ski classes are held, take place during the summer months. Again details can be obtained from the National Ski Federation.

Additional simulated ski-ing

There are several different kinds of apparatus available for use by skiers as aids to ski-ing preparation. Some of these devices are small and just require a little floor space where the skier stands on the spot and performs a rhythmic exercise. One of the largest machines which produces 'endless ski-ing' is the Mogulscope, using a wide endless mat with a low friction surface, on which the skier stands in the same position while the slope moves under the mini-skis. While this simulated ski-ing is more akin to running down the wrong way of an escalator, it has the advantage that instruction and guidance of the pupil can

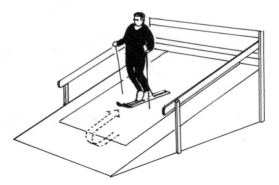

Figure 58. 'Mogul' ski slope – continuous revolving mat.

144

be given from a closeup position. The instructor is able to hold the pupil and move the pupil into feeling correct ski-ing stances over the skis.

While artificial slopes and other machines may not be entirely like the feel of snow, anything that will give a ski-type exercise is good.

7 · Going Ski-ing – Where and How

Where can you go ski-ing? . . . and when is the best time? . . . and what's the best way of getting there? The answers are that you can ski almost anywhere where there are mountains and hills that have snowfall, that ski-ing is possible all the year round, and that you can arrange your ski holiday under your own steam or go with a party.

The Alps are still the most popular mountain area for the ski enthusiast, with the long tradition of providing facilities for all tastes. Norway and Sweden have their own special attractions, and Scotland too can offer a good winter holiday. Outside of Europe, the hills and mountains of North America have seen tremendous developments of hundreds of ski areas to cater for the keen U.S. and Canadian skiers. Japan too has developed many ski areas, and with over five million skiers will be an interesting place to go and take a ski holiday. In the southern hemisphere, Australia, New Zealand and the Andes of South America all have very good ski areas, with many excellent potential snows for the future.

As for the best time to take your winter sports holiday, it depends on what you want to do on your holiday. If you want the traditional ski holiday of powder snow, après-ski entertainment, etc., then Christmas through to February is the time, with March and April giving you more sunshine with less powder snow! The length of the ski season at a ski resort is directly connected with its altitude. At some ski resorts you can ski all the year round, as against those places that are not so high where ski-ing is only possible for the three winter months.

Getting to your ski resort and arranging the holiday is made very easy by the travel agent. Complete packaged holidays offer very good value without the bother of having to make all the separate travel, hotel booking, ski hire, lesson and lift ticket arrangements yourself. Joining a party or a group has much to offer, as ski-ing is a very friendly sport that quickly breaks down barriers and reserve in people. If you decide to go by your own means, driving your car directly to the snows, it will need a little preparation, although having your own transport can be very useful at some of the larger ski resorts.

Choosing a ski resort – consideration factors

Having an adequate snow coverage is an obvious requirement for any ski resort. But although winter is regarded as being the period from November to April, it is impossible to guarantee that skiable snow will always be available during this time. Changing weather cycles can influence the snowfall, either over a whole continent or affecting the amount of snow that may fall in just local pocket areas. It has been known for a winter to start with heavy falls of snow in November and December, followed by very little snowfall after that, causing the ski season to close earlier than usual. Just as fickle can be the winter when there is no real depth of snow until the end of January. Then it may come down in huge quantities that cause extreme avalanche danger so that the good ski-ing is closed off.

Predominantly northerly winds bring sufficient depth of snow to mountain areas from 1,200 metres above sea level by mid-December, and although it is impossible to predict a set pattern of weather and snowfall, the best snow conditions usually occur from the end of January right through February. The ideal month for a ski holiday can be March when snow

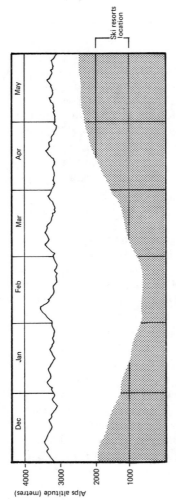

Figure 59. Snow cover of Alps in winter.

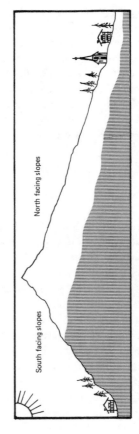

Figure 60. Section of an Alp – snow cover.

conditions have settled down and the sun is warm and the weather too can be more pleasant. By April, the snow lying on south facing slopes can be bare and patchy, retreating up to 2,400 metres, while other slopes are still covered in good spring snow.

The general topography of a ski resort can affect the degree of snow depth. South facing slopes collect less snow than the more gentle angled slopes with a northerly facing aspect, and a careful look at a particular resort's geographic layout is well worth while – runs that are not directly facing the sun will stay in better condition than those which are subject to direct melt from the sun's rays and then freeze up solid after a cold night.

Most Alpine resorts have been developed from villages that existed before ski-ing came into being a winter sport. The hard working hill-farmers were not thinking of finding good ski slopes when they first settled in the valleys and grassy alps, so consequently some villages nestling deep in alpine valleys do not have suitable slopes immediately adjacent to them. Ski resorts have to have an altitude of at least 800 metres, and, depending on their geographic location, the altitude will influence the length of the resort's season.

In the Alps and North American mountain areas, there are now several new 'created ski centres', that have been built specifically for ski-ing. These new 'ski villages' have been located because of their good ski slopes and reliable snow conditions. Most of these new centres lie at 1,600 metres or above this height, with very carefully planned ski runs and lift systems to make the maximum use of the terrain for all grades of ski-ing.

Another factor to be considered when choosing a resort is its nearness to major population centres. Weekend crowds can make for huge lift queues at popular ski resorts within easy reach of big cities.

If the cost of your holiday has to be carefully considered, it is worth comparing the prices that hotels offer from the low-season (colder January and February period) to the high-season (Christmas and the popular March and April period). You may then find that you can afford to ski at a better class resort during the less crowded low-season time.

Where to go

While the person who can ski well will be looking for the best challenge and variety of ski-ing that a resort can offer, the beginner should be careful in the choice of a ski centre.

The absolute beginner should ensure that the resort has adequate nursery slopes, preferably next to the village and not part of a busy ski run that finishes through the beginners' area. Check also that there are ski-tows specially located for the use of learner skiers, and that there are easy ski pistes for you to tackle. You may also find that you will want a rest from ski-ing all the time, and so a resort should have alternative attractions such as swimming, ski bobbing, skating and curling to make a change from struggling with skis.

Austria

The numerous small ski villages are popular with beginners and intermediate skiers. Lift facilities are good, and ski schools offer excellent tuition with many instructors speaking at least 'ski English'. Unfortunately many of the picturesque villages are below 1,000 metres, and can be short of snow in a 'dry' winter. The natural gaiety of the Austrians makes for very good après-ski entertainment, as well as the fact that for Austria ski-ing is a major economic industry.

France

In order to meet the growing demands of winter sports holiday-makers, the French Government has sponsored the development of several created ski centres. These brand new ski resorts offer excellent value to both the good skier and the learner. All established French resorts have first-class ski schools, although instruction in English may be difficult to find. Like all sports, ski-ing is taken very seriously in France, and there are plans to make sure that there are adequate ski lifts and inter-linking runs throughout the ski resorts. In keeping with the efforts to make the French Alps a leader in modern ski-ing development, there are several ski schools that teach the short ski method of learning to ski. Features of all French resorts are the well-groomed pistes and organised safety ski patrols.

Italy

Apart from the established sophisticated ski resorts, there are many new smaller villages developing their ski-ing potential. Prices are generally cheaper than the neighbouring Alpine countries, and the resorts are very relaxed and informal. Journey times from airports to some of the more out of the way centres can be long bus rides.

Switzerland

The tradition of providing ski-ing facilities of a high standard as well as reliable service is what you pay for at Swiss resorts. The large élite resorts have excellent snowfields among the high Alps that offer some of the best ski-ing in the world. During the high-season, the more popular resorts can suffer from overcrowding, especially where access cable cars or mountain railways have not been enlarged to provide greater uphill transport capacity.

Spain

Rapidly developing its high snowy mountains, Spain offers very good value for money. Snow conditions can vary, and some of the areas suffer from high winds, but with development progress many very good created ski centres will make Spain a more attractive proposition for ski holidays.

Norway

Where ski-ing began, the tradition of cross-country ski-ing remains favourite with many Norwegians, although much has been done to provide lift-served Alpine-type downhill ski-ing on the gentler slopes. There is a natural friendliness to English-speaking visitors, and this with the informal atmosphere of Norwegian hospitality makes for very pleasant ski-ing. Gentle slopes, the reliable snows of a Nordic winter, and good ski schools make for excellent ski-ing for the beginner and intermediate skier. With the revived interest in cross-country or trail ski-ing as a more relaxing form of enjoying the sport, Norway offers endless touring possibilities.

Scotland

The Highland mountains of Scotland offer the best ski-ing to be had in Britain, and should in no way whatsoever be compared with any ski-ing that can be had in the Alps or Scandinavia. Notorious fickle weather can make or break the limited ski-ing available. The strong gales and blizzards fill in the natural 'corries' or mountain gullies with snow, forming ski-runs in a good winter several feet deep, and extending the season on firm spring snow sometimes into June. In spite of the weather, ski schools give the beginner and intermediate a good grounding in ski technique. In a good snow season, the weather and spring snow conditions are best from March onwards, but be prepared for long queue lines during weekends and school holiday periods.

Getting value for your money

The cost of a ski holiday varies greatly, depending on where and how you go. The packaged holiday arrangement gives the best value with regard to having the least amount of fuss and bother with travel arrangements and extra payments for ski rental, ski lessons and lift tickets. However, you are committed to a restricted choice of hotels and dates, that may not fit in with your requirements and you may have to book as an individual. If this is the case, then enquire for air or rail travel fare concessions that may be available. Be prepared when booking under any arrangement, to have to pay extra for baths, drinks and insurance. Joining a party in a chalet, or even booking your own chalet is a very enjoyable way of having a ski holiday. Above all, collect all the reputable ski travel brochures and shop around for the best value.

Taking children

Taking small children on a ski holiday can present problems unless you have adequately prepared the requirements to ensure that they will be well looked after. If you have a young family it is worth considering a resort that has a kindergarten or crèche, where you can leave children while you enjoy your ski-ing. One question frequently asked by parents is 'At what age do you start children ski-ing?' Some children can become fairly mobile at the age of three; that is they can walk around and climb up and slide down gentle slopes. Until the age of about seven, ski-ing is just another game, and so long as they are warm and waterproof, most youngsters will stay out for about two hours playing this sliding-downhill game. It is worth noting that most ski schools put a minimum age limit on children accepted into classes – a small tot that has to be constantly picked up out of the snow by the instructor can ruin the ski session for the other kids!

Once a child has got his ski legs, and they come naturally to most, then from about the age of eight upwards all you will have to do is ensure that he has his lift ticket securely fastened on, and that's the last you will see of him until he comes back starving with hunger.

Always check that the child's bindings and retaining straps are in good order, and don't forget that a liberal smear of sun cream is always necessary to protect the youngster's sensitive skin. In choosing a resort suitable for children, perhaps the smaller village ski resorts are those where they may feel more at home.

Going by car

Driving out to your ski resort can have several advantages that outweigh the inconvenience of the long journey needed to get there initially. By having your own transport, it is possible to stay at cheaper accommodation just outside the resort, taking a short drive up to ski each day. At some of the large ski centres it is a great advantage to have a car in order to ski at all the different areas easily, and even nearby ski resorts. Should the weather or snow conditions change for the worse in your particular resort, you can take off and search out better ski-ing. For the better skier, having a car with you means that you are able to get a greater variety of ski-ing during a holiday than would be possible by using only public transport. Most Alpine roads are kept clear of snow by efficient ploughing, but you should carry chains as a precaution. On some of the winding passes or access roads, the police will not allow cars to proceed unless equipped with wheel chains or special snow tyres. When driving on packed snow never over-rev the engine and cause wheel spin; only the minimum of power is required to turn the driving wheels and retain traction. At the same time it is useful to carry a small shovel and a bag of sand just to help you get out of trouble, if you get bogged down. When climbing a gradient on snowy or ice-covered roads, always leave plenty of space in between your car and the next one, so that if the latter gets stuck after losing traction on the slippery surface, you have a chance to avoid it and not get stuck yourself. It is easy enough to get adequate information from the various motoring associations as to the best way to winterize your car – such things as the correct amount of anti-freeze solutions in cooling systems, tyres, and the fitting of an engine warming device are necessary.

Carrying skis will require a suitable rack, and any ski shop will be able to supply this. Very useful is a ski rack that can be locked so that the skis can be left on the roof in safety. Place the skis with the tips to the rear, and it is a good idea to put them in covers for a long journey, so as to prevent road dirt or salt-laden spray attacking the metal exposed parts of the skis and bindings.

As well as being able to carry extra clothing and equipment, you can also take other passengers and so help to share the cost of the journey. If costs are being shared it may be worth considering taking the car by air ferry to cut down on time and the length of the drive.

155

8 · The Sporting Side of Ski-ing

Competitive ski-ing

Ski racing has been much a part of ski-ing right from the very beginning of the sport. The development of ski technique and equipment is directly associated with the racers' search for ways and means to go faster, under better control and safety. In the early days, ski racing was very much a relaxed and, to a certain extent, an informal affair, with sometimes only several seconds in time separating the winners. Now it is a highly organised sport controlled by the F.I.S. where the racer has to graduate through several categories of racing standards before reaching international level. To stand a chance of reaching the top level, the skier has to start in the junior grading races and, through a points allocation system on the results of racing performance, can only then go through the various classifications before reaching the A class top standard. All this requires a tremendous amount of hard work, training, travel to events, cost of equipment and dedication, in order to get anywhere near to competing internationally.

There are, fortunately, many races held for the person who wants to have a go just for the fun of it. Ski clubs organise their own races, set on courses that enable all the entrants to enjoy a taste of racing without the pressures of the 'big league events'. Some ski schools also stage a weekly fun race for the school patrons, and these events can be just as exciting as a big international event, especially as nearly everyone receives a prize for competing!

Junior training programmes

In order to train potential future racers, most countries have special programmes catering for the training of juniors, starting from midgets aged 8 or 9, through to age 16 or 17. In Britain the organising bodies are the National Ski Federation and the Scottish National Ski Council, who undertake a careful plan of training sessions and full race promotion both at home and in the Alps.

The races

Racing is a very complex subject, requiring the whole of a separate book to describe fully every detail, but just to give the onlooker an idea of the basic differences, the three main events are described as follows.

The Downhill race

This is a high speed course of anything up to $3\frac{1}{2}$ miles long, having long run outs and sharp drops over different changes in terrain. The control 'gates' are set wide apart, and serve primarily as a means of marking the main corridor of the course rather than as obstacles in themselves. The fastest time down the course takes the winning place, and so the ideal is to take the shortest possible line, keeping the skis on the snow for speed, and maintaining an aerodynamic crouched position to reduce wind resistance for as long as possible. Competitors start at set time intervals, usually one minute apart, and can reach a speed of over 60 m.p.h. Understandably, crash helmets are compulsory wear.

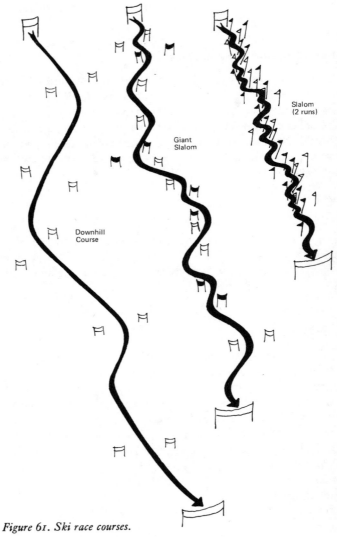

Slalom
(2 runs)

Giant
Slalom

Downhill
Course

Figure 61. Ski race courses.

The Slalom race

Slalom racing takes place over two courses of from 40 to 75 'gates' on each course. The gates are set fairly close together in various combinations, to challenge the racer's turning and reaction ability. Each gate consists of two coloured flags and poles set approx. $3\frac{1}{2}$ metres apart, and the racer's boots have to pass through a line drawn between each pole in order to avoid disqualification. The gates are placed in basically two different ways – an 'open' gate where the poles are placed horizontally across the slope, and a 'closed' gate with the poles placed vertically up the slope. A colour order of blue, red and yellow gates is followed through the whole pattern and all the combinations of the course. The racer with the best time wins over the combined results of the two runs. Because timing is so critical, with fractions of a second separating the winners, electronic starting and finishing timing devices are now used in major events.

The Giant Slalom race

The Giant Slalom course is set with gates of a wider width apart, two poles hold the flag on each side of the gate, and they are arranged in a colour order of blue and red gates. The courses are longer than a slalom race, combining some of the speed of downhill racing with the turning control required in the tighter setting of slalom racing.

Proficiency tests

Many skiers like to have some idea of their ability on skis without resorting to the role of becoming racers, and to encourage the challenge of becoming more expert in ski technique, there have been several testing schemes in use over the years. The Ski Club of Great Britain have carried out their own tests in various Alpine resorts since the beginning of the century. Their awards are of Bronze, Silver and Gold medals both for technical standard of ski-ing and for the ability to ski downhill on the piste and in difficult snow conditions. Recently the National Ski Federation have organised a Junior Testing Scheme under sponsorship from Coca-Cola, where young skiers can be tested from the elementary basic ski-ing stage into the first taste of Slalom racing. These tests will be eventually run for adults as well, similar to the Molstar and Nastar tests run in North America, where the participant is awarded according to the percentage of time allowance given over the course from the Vorlaufer's time.

British Junior Alpine ski tests

Conducted by officials of the National Ski Federation and qualified ski schools, for skiers under the age of 18 years, on snow or artificial slopes in Great Britain, or the Alps and Norway.

One Star Test
1. Climbing side-step.
2. Descent. Straight schuss.
3. Snowplough glide descent to a controlled stop.
4. Diagonal traverse to left and right.
5. Right and left linked snowplough turn and stop.
6. Ski educational questions (taken from Ski education leaflet provided with entry form).

Two Star Test
1. Direct controlled side-slip of at least 5 metres in either direction.

2. Diagonal controlled side-slip of at least 5 metres in either direction.
3. Four consecutive stem-Christiania turns to left and right.
4. Swing to the hill from a traverse to left and right.
5. Non-stop no fall descent through at least 6 open gates.
6. Stop turns from a schuss to left and right.
7. Ski educational questions.

Three Star Test
1. At least 30 gate Slalom. Candidates must be within 20 per cent of the Vorlaufer's time.
2. No fall non-stop downhill run of at least 300 metres on a piste. Candidates must be within 20 per cent of the Vorlaufer's time.
3. Ski educational questions.

Address of the National Ski Federation of Great Britain
118 Eaton Square, London SW1.

Glossary of Ski-ing Terms

Angulation – sideways bending of the body in relation to the stance over the skis.

Anticipation – pre-turning or twisting movement by the skier, before the turn starts.

Avalement – ski-ing manoeuvre using extremes of leg bending and folding over bumps.

Avalanche – snow slide (G) Lawine.

Basket – the snow ring on the end of a ski pole.

Basic swing – an elementary ski turn using the snowplough and parallel skid.

Beginner – a novice skier (F) débutant, (G) Anfanger.

Binding – the mechanical means of attaching the ski boot to the ski.

Bum bag – a waist bag for carrying lunch, sunglasses, cream, etc.

Camber – the built-in curve along the ski sole.

Chairlift – seated uphill transport (F) Telesiege, (G) Sesselbahn.

Christiania – a turn or swing to change direction with the skis parallel.

Compression (or Compensation) *turns* – folding the legs to compensate for bumps.

Counter rotation – turning the upper part of the body in the opposite direction to the ski turn.

Cross-country – (trail ski-ing) ski touring across undulating country.

Downsink – bending of the knees and ankles into a part-kneeling position.

Downhill race – ski race straight downhill through wide controlling gates.

Edges – the steel edges fixed to the sides of the ski's running surface (F) carres, (G) Kanten.

Egg position – streamlined crouching position over the skis for speed.

Fall-line – the steepest line down a slope.

F.I.S. – Federation Internationale de Ski, world body organising competition ski-ing.

Flex – the degree of bending in a ski along its length.

Gates – controlling passages for racing, made with poles and flags.

Gefahr – (G) danger, used on ski run markers and avalanche-prone slopes.

Gesperrt – (G) closed, (F) fermé.

Giant Slalom – race course where the controlling gates are set in wide turns.

G.L.M. – Graduated Length Method of using various lengths of ski in learning.

Herringbone – climbing step with feet and skis splayed out in a V form.

Hot-dogging – acrobatic and free style ski-ing events.

Inner ski – the ski on the inside of the turning arc.

Inside edge – the edge of the ski under the inside of the boot.

Jet turn – advanced parallel turn using a 'jetting' forward action of the feet.

Jump turn – turn made by jumping both skis off the snow.

Kick turn – a standing turn made by lifting or 'kicking' one ski round in the opposite direction.

Lower ski – the ski on the downhill side.

Mogul – term applied to the bumps formed on ski runs.

Outside edge – edge of the ski on the outside of the boot.
Outside ski – the ski on the outside of the turning arc.

Piste – a ski run or trail.
Pole plant – placing of the ski pole into the snow as an aid to turning control.

Schuss – ski-ing straight downhill.
Short skis – skis of length shorter than head height.
Sideslip – flattening the skis and skidding them sideways down the slope (F) glisser, (G) rutschen.
Ski-bob – a type of ski bicycle.
Ski-doo – a motorised type of ski-scooter.
Slalom – a ski race through closely placed gates in various combinations of setting.
Snowplough – a position over the skis where the legs are opened out with the skis in a V form from the tips (F) chasse-niege, (G) Schneepflug.
Sole – the underside or running surface of a ski.
Spring snow (Corn snow) – old weathered snow that has compacted down into small ice crystals.
Stem – the action of opening out one ski at an angle to the other from the tip.
Swing – turning action when the skis are skidded round parallel to one another.

Traverse – ski-ing across the slope (F) traversée, (G) Schrägfahrt.
Turn – changing direction in a curving line when ski-ing downhill.

Unweighting – momentarily taking the weight off the skis to assist turning action.

Upmotion – a movement by the skier by straightening or stretching upwards.

Upper ski – the ski on the uphill side.

Vorlage – leaning forward on the skis.

Wedeln – short linked turns by successive rhythmic leg play.

Weight change – transferring the weight pressure from one ski to the other.

Wellen technique – ski technique for ski-ing round and turning on bumpy terrain.